Lincoln Slept Here

Lincoln Slept Here

LINCOLN FAMILY SITES IN AMERICA

Abraham Lincoln's
Illinois Years 1830-1861

Edward Steers, Jr.

DESIGNED BY Kieran McAuliffe

DEDICATION

*This work is respectfully dedicated
to the National Park Service and its employees
in their more than 100 year of service
helping to preserve our history and heritage
and enriching the lives of all.
Thank you.*

School children pose with "The Resolute Lincoln" the statue by Avard Fairbanks at New Salem State Historic Site. The statue was given to the state of Illinois by the National Society of the Sons of Utah Pioneers in 1954.

Lincoln Slept Here

Abraham Lincoln's Illinois Years 1830-1861

Table of Contents

PREFACE

On February 12, 1830, Abraham Lincoln turned twenty-one, achieving what legal experts termed "his majority." Lincoln was no longer bound to his parents by law and could set out on his own, a free man. From the beginning of written history, around 3100 BC, the concept that children were legally bound to their parents was both unwritten and written law. The concept known as the "age of majority" stated that children were not legally independent of their parents in all matters until the age of twenty-one. Until then they were considered "infants" in the eyes of the law. In 1830, the United States followed English Common Law, setting the age of majority at twenty-one years for both sexes. To use a term Abraham Lincoln would clearly understand, the age of majority was when a minor child became emancipated under the law.

For much of his youth, Lincoln worked for or under the direction of his father. On occasion, Lincoln was farmed out, rented some would say, to work for a neighbor at his father's direction. This included hard manual labor, associated with farming on the frontier. Forests had to be clear-cut of trees; stumps pulled from their roots, fields plowed, rails split, and crops planted and harvested, something Lincoln was good at, but disliked. He considered using his brain to be superior to using his brawn. He was not lazy, by any stretch of the imagination, just opposed to menial work. While Lincoln disliked menial labor, he respected those whose only means of labor was with a strong back and sweat.

Thomas Lincoln
Lincoln Memorial University,
Harrogate, Tennessee.

Using the third person, Lincoln wrote an autobiography for John Locke Scripps in the campaign of 1860 in which he said:

He [Lincoln] settled in an unbroken forest; and the clearing away of surplus wood was the great task at hand. A, though very young, was large for his age and had an axe put into his hands at once; and from that time till within his twenty-third year, he was constantly handling that most useful instrument – less, of course, in plowing and harvesting seasons.

Lincoln spoke sparingly of his father and often in a disparaging manner, but others did not, as were the descriptions of his birth and early life in "mudsill" conditions of poverty meant to contrast his poor upbringing with his success, so too were the disparaging descriptions of his relationship with his father aimed at showing Lincoln rising despite his "mistreatment." Lincoln historian Michael Burlingame wrote, "Thomas rented his

boy." And later, "Lincoln was virtually a slave toiling as butcher, ferry operator, river man, store clerk, farmhand, wood chopper, distiller, and sawyer earning anywhere from ten cents to thirty-one cents a day. He handed these meager wages over to Thomas [his father] in compliance with the law stipulating that children were the property of their father, and that any money they earned belonged to him … locked in bondage, Abraham felt as if he were a chattel on a Southern plantation." Burlingame seems to use the widely accepted practices of the day to establish a thorough dislike of Lincoln for his father.

English-born intellectual Christopher Hitchens (who became an American citizen in 2007) mirrored Burlingame's view of the father-son relationship when he wrote in his *Atlantic* review of Burlingame's two-volume biography of Lincoln, "The cruelty and degeneracy Lincoln was subjected to in his youth forged his iron will." Such polemics simply do not square with other accounts of the two men's relationship. That Lincoln was forced to turn over his "meager wages" to his father is assumed, but even if true, does not support the idea that Lincoln was "locked in bondage." If this were the case, virtually all of the frontier youth were "locked in bondage" to their fathers.

That a certain strain existed between the father and son is true, but not anywhere to the level some would like us to believe. And, Lincoln's relationship with his father did not "forge his iron will." Lincoln was ambitious, self-reliant, and smarter than anyone in the surrounding community, including his father. He was anxious to set out and establish a life of his own. This does not mean he was abused and sought to escape a father he hated.

Although free to leave his parents in March 1830, Lincoln chose to help them move one more time to the fertile prairie of Illinois. Moving to the Decatur area from Indiana in March, Lincoln helped his father build their new cabin home on the banks of the Sangamon River. This is not the act of a son who hates his father.

Lincoln remained in Decatur until the following March 1831, a full year after he was free to set out on his own. That winter of 1831 was particularly brutal with four-foot snow blizzards and sub-zero temperatures. Known as the winter of the "deep snow," the Lincoln family hunkered down until the March thaw. With the coming of spring and having helped establish his parents in their new home, Lincoln decided to exercise his right as an independent agent and move out on his own.

His big break came when John Hanks, his cousin

who had lured his father to the Decatur area, was visited by a rascally entrepreneur named Denton Offutt. Hanks later recalled that Offutt wanted Hanks to "run a flatboat for him," to New Orleans. Hanks, unable to do it alone, went to see the Lincolns in their Decatur home and asked Lincoln and his stepbrother, John D. Johnston, if they wanted to join the venture. Hanks told the two young men that Offutt would pay them "50 [cents] per day plus $60 for the trip to New Orleans." It was a generous offer. The two jumped at the opportunity. It was just what Lincoln was looking for to begin his life anew.

And so Lincoln set out from his family, only to visit them on rare occasions over the next twenty years. The trip to New Orleans introduced him to the village of New Salem when the flatboat became caught on the milldam that powered the local gristmill. The story of Lincoln's rescue of the boat from the dam and his saving Offutt's cargo launched his career. Following Lincoln's return from New Orleans, Offutt offered him the job of running his store. Lincoln would accept and spend the next six

years maturing into the man that would one day save the nation, and forever change the course of history.

New Salem was something of an epiphany for Lincoln. It was as if someone suddenly threw a light switch flooding the darkness with light. Growing up mostly as a somewhat isolated farmboy, Lincoln found himself surrounded by friendly people. As the great Lincoln historian Benjamin Thomas wrote in his little monograph on New Salem, "It was at New Salem that Abraham Lincoln for the first time learned to live with people." New Salem was the first organized community in which Lincoln played a major role. He rose from a wandering straggler to a community leader.

From farm laborer to president, Lincoln passed through postmaster, surveyor, lawyer, state legislator, and congressman. He read Burns and Shakespeare for intellectual enjoyment and studied law. Most of all, he learned about people, their dreams and their tragedies, and developed an empathy for the unfortunate. The lessons stuck and opened his heart to a wide, wide world.

Flatboating on the Mississippi River. Alfred Waud.

*At twenty one I came to Illinois,
and passed the first year in Macon County.
Then I got to New-Salem...*
Abraham Lincoln

The Rail Splitter J. L. G. Ferris

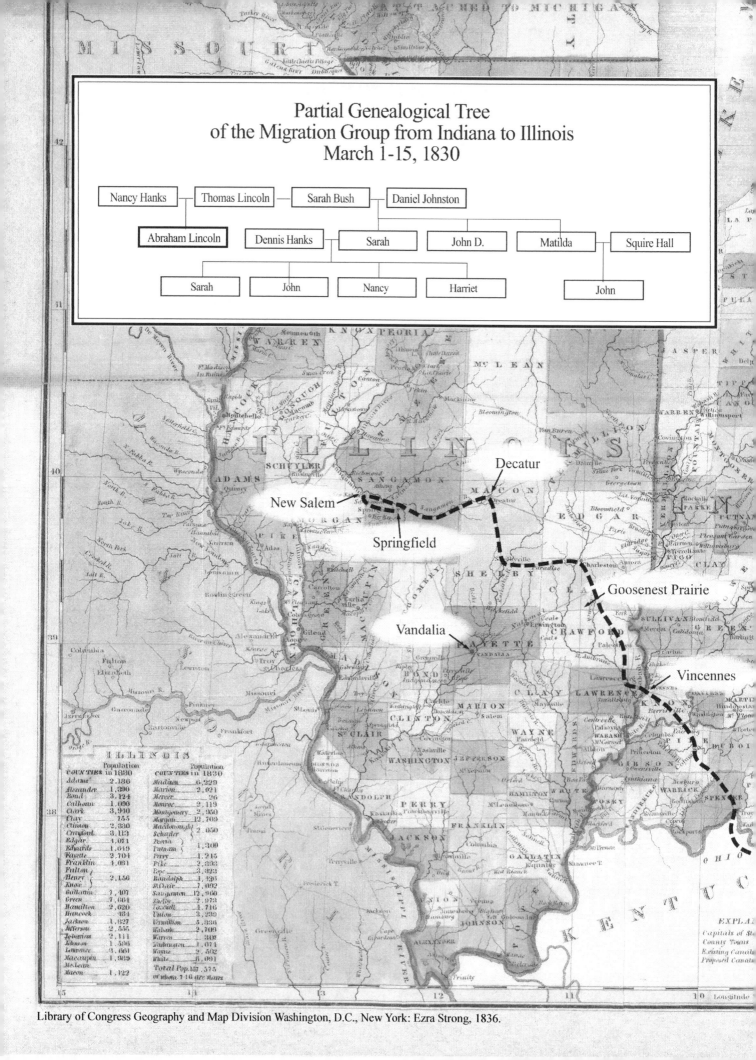

Partial Genealogical Tree
of the Migration Group from Indiana to Illinois
March 1-15, 1830

Nancy Hanks — Thomas Lincoln — Sarah Bush — Daniel Johnston

Abraham Lincoln | Dennis Hanks | Sarah | John D. | Matilda | Squire Hall

Sarah | John | Nancy | Harriet | John

Decatur

New Salem

Springfield

Goosenest Prairie

Vandalia

Vincennes

Decatur
1830-1834

In 1828, John Hanks, Nancy Hanks's cousin and a close friend of Thomas Lincoln, pulled up stakes and left Indiana for the fertile prairie of central Illinois. Two years later he lured Thomas Lincoln from his Indiana home to join him. Thomas and his family had experienced an epidemic of fever, known as the ague (malarial fever), along with a resurgence of the milk sickness that had killed Nancy Lincoln in 1818. Deciding one epidemic was enough, Thomas Lincoln decided to join his first wife's cousin in Illinois.

The land was rich and affordable, and Thomas intended to squat on the land the first year before committing to buying the land. John Hanks selected a tract of land not far from his own and began preparing logs in anticipation of Thomas's arrival. The migration would be the ninth of Thomas's life and the fifth as a married man since his first home with Nancy in Elizabethtown, Kentucky. This time the migration would include the families of Dennis Hanks and John Hall, a total of thirteen people who would make the two hundred mile journey from Indiana to Illinois. Along with Thomas and Sarah Bush Lincoln were Abraham and John D. Johnston; Sarah Elizabeth Johnston Hanks, her

Thomas Lincoln purchased a team of oxen to pull the large wagon carrying the worldly goods of the three families the two hundred miles to Illinois. The caravan, consisting of thirteen people, two ox-drawn wagons, and one horse-drawn wagon, crossed the Wabash river into Illinois on March 6, 1830.

husband Dennis, and their four children (Sarah Jane, John Talbot, Nancy Ann, and Harriett), and Matilda Johnston Hall, her husband Squire Hall, and their infant son John.

The trip took fifteen days, from March 1 to March 15, and occurred during two weeks of freezing, wet weather that plagued the group throughout the journey. The main obstacle was the Wabash River that formed part of the eastern boundary between Indiana and Illinois. The exact point where the caravan crossed the river comes from Lincoln himself who related the circumstances of that crossing to a fellow Republican in 1860. At the Republican state convention in May of that year, one of the delegates, Peter Smith, wrote a letter home to his cousin in which he told of a conversation he had with Lincoln. Smith wrote that he asked Lincoln if he were the same man that had crossed the Wabash River at Vincennes, passing through Lawrenceville, Illinois, thirty years earlier in the dead of winter barefoot. Lincoln replied:

> About thirty years ago I did drive my father's ox wagon [sic] and team moving my father's family through your town of Lawrenceville and I was afoot but not barefoot. In my young days I frequently went barefooted but on that occasion I had on a substantial pair of shoes – it was a cold day in March and I never went barefooted in cold weather. I will remember that trip thro' your County as long as I live. I crossed the Wabash at Vincennes and the river being high the road on the low prairie was covered with water a half mile at a stretch and the water covered with ice – the only means by which I could keep on the road was by observing the stakes on each side placed as guides when the water is over the road. When I came to the water I put a favorite dog I had along into the waggon and got in myself and whipped up my oxen and started into the water to pick my way across as well as I

could – after breaking the ice and wading about 1/4 of a mile my little dog jumped out of the waggon and the ice being thin he broke through and was struggling for life. I could not bear to lose my dog and I jumped out of the waggon and waded waist deep in the ice and water, got hold of him and helped him out and saved him.

With his little dog shivering from the icy water, but safe, Lincoln and the caravan headed for Decatur near the center of the state approximately thirty miles east of Springfield. Arriving on March 15, 1830, at the home of John Hanks they rested for a day before heading out to the site that Hanks had selected for them. It was located approximately ten miles west of the town of Decatur on a bluff overlooking a bend in the Sangamon River. Here they found a supply of cut logs prepared by John Hanks ready to use in building their new Illinois home. In 1904, members of the Daughters of the American Revolution (DAR) erected a stone memorial identifying the believed site of the cabin. Unfortunately, they missed the exact location by over twelve hundred feet. The actual site is believed to be on a bluff overlooking the Sangamon River, as a result of archaeological investigations conducted by the state of Illinois. The new site, commemorated with a stone monument, has become the Lincoln Trail Homestead State Park.

The men quickly went to work erecting cabins for

Lincoln as a young teenager with his dog. Statue by Paul Manship for Lincoln National Life Foundation. Artist's model at Lincoln Memorial University, Harrogate, Tennessee.

Left: Stone marker placed at the believed site of the Lincoln cabin in Lincoln Homestead Park.
Right: *Stone marker placed in 1904 at the then believed site of the Lincoln cabin by the Daughters of the American Revolution.*

John and Dennis Hanks standing in front of the Decatur cabin.

Broadside advertising Lincoln's first home in Illinois. Philadelphia was the last stop for the cabin before it presumably disappeared at sea.

their families and Abraham, along with cousin John Hanks, set about splitting enough rails to fence a ten acre field. Thirty years later, John Hanks would gain a modicum of fame for himself and his now famous cousin by marching into the Republican Convention in Decatur carrying a rail he claimed was split by Lincoln on the Decatur farm, instantly giving rise to "The Railsplitter" candidate. In his autobiographical sketch for John Locke Scripps, Lincoln wrote about the convention stunt: "These are, or are supposed to be, the rails about which so much is being said just now, though these are far from being the first or only rails ever made by Abraham."

Abandoned in 1831, the cabin was still in use at the time of Lincoln's death in 1865. Within a few weeks of Lincoln's assassination, John Hanks purchased the cabin and, together with Dennis Hanks, dismantled it and took it on tour. Exhibited in Chicago, Boston, New York (at P. T. Barnum's New American Museum), and Philadelphia, it was allegedly sold to an English syndicate and lost at sea during shipment to England.

In 1975, after considerable haggling and struggling over funds to complete an adequate memorial at the home site, the Decatur Kiwanis Club pledged $15,000 toward

Replica cabin erected in 1975 at the Lincoln Homestead Park. The cabin was ultimately destroyed by fire caused by vandals.

completion of a reconstructed log cabin. Historian James Hickey, curator of the Lincoln Collection in the Illinois State Historical Library, served as a consultant on the construction of the cabin. Unfortunately, the cabin was destroyed by fire set by vandals in 1989 and again in 1990. The cabin remains were removed and the DAR memorial stone relocated to the current cabin site.

The summer of 1830 saw fever once again spread through the area around Decatur. By December, the community suffered the worst snowstorms and freezing weather in anyone's memory. Thomas Lincoln, discouraged by both events, decided to return to Indiana and abandon Illinois. But, on retracing his steps back along the route to Indiana he was persuaded by an old friend to give Illinois another chance, this time at a place

called Buck Grove. Thomas squatted on the land until his move to Goosenest Prairie where he settled on an eighty-acre farm.

On February 12, 1830, Lincoln celebrated his twenty-first birthday. He had reached his majority and, according to the law in most states, was free to take leave of his father and stepmother. In March, 1831, after helping build the Decatur cabin he bid his father and mother goodbye and set out on his own. His ambition had been burning for some time, and he was more than ready to seek his own way in the world. With Thomas and Sarah settled in their new home, Lincoln set out with no real sense of where he was going or how he would get there, but he was determined to begin a life of his own.

The Lincoln cabin as represented by John and Dennis Hanks. From a heavily retouched carte de visite photograph taken in 1865 thirty-four years after Thomas Lincoln abandoned the home site for Goosenest Prairie.

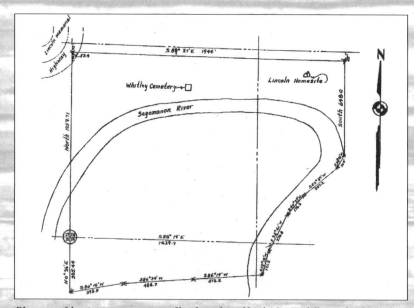

Plat map of the sixty-two acre tract of land purchased by the State of Illinois for the Lincoln Homestead Park. An Archaeological and Architectural Assessment of the Lincoln Cabin, Rural Macon County, Illinois, *(Decatur, IL: Fever River Research, 2009).*

Goosenest Prairie
1831-1869
The last stop for Thomas
and Sarah Lincoln

The first year in Illinois proved to be among the harshest years for the new immigrants. In the fall of 1830, several members of the three families contracted a peculiar kind of illness known as the ague, a malaria-like fever marked by spasms of chills, fever, and sweating that recur at regular intervals. Compounding their troubles was the terrible winter of 1830-1831. It was remembered throughout the state as the winter of the "deep snow." After months of suffering and privation, Thomas Lincoln and his extended family decided to return to their home in Indiana where living had proved to be much better than their first year in Illinois.

Instead of returning to Indiana, however, Thomas was persuaded to settle in Coles County close to friends rather than abandon their new state. From 1831 until 1834, the couple lived in a cabin that set near thirty miles to the southeast of their Decatur home. It was the first of three homes in Coles County, Illinois,

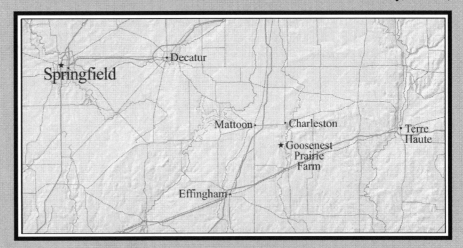

and their second home in Illinois.

In 1834 Thomas Lincoln purchased his third tract of land, a forty-acre farm where he built his third log cabin in just four years. The couple lived here until 1840 when they moved for the fourth and last time to a farm near the Embarras River at Goosenest Prairie on the southern edge of Coles County. Thomas bought eighty acres of land from a neighbor, Reuben Moore.

Constructed of two cabins joined by a large fireplace, the cabin was home to as many as 18 members of the Lincoln and Johnston families. It was the last farm for both Thomas and Sarah. Thomas died in 1851 and Sarah in 1869. While no record exists showing that Abraham Lincoln ever visited his parents at their first two Coles County farms, he made several visits to the Goosenest Prairie site. Throughout the period of Thomas and Sarah's lives at Goosenest Prairie, Lincoln provided financial help on several occasions. At the time of his nomination as the Republican candidate for president, Lincoln made one last visit to Coles County where he spent the night with his stepmother at a friend's house where the two reminisced about the

past. It would be their last visit together. Sarah Lincoln died in 1869, four years after her beloved stepson.

In 1893, the cabin was disassembled and displayed at the World's Columbian Exposition in Chicago, Illinois. Following the Exposition the cabin was lost, its fate unknown. An exact replica was built in 1934, using photographs and contemporary descriptions by the Civilian Conservation Corps. The Lincoln Log Cabin State Historic Site consists of a farmstead nearly identical to the Lincoln's actual farm.

Rear view of the cabin at Goosenest Prairie.

Front view of the original cabin of Thomas Lincoln at Goosenest Prairie.

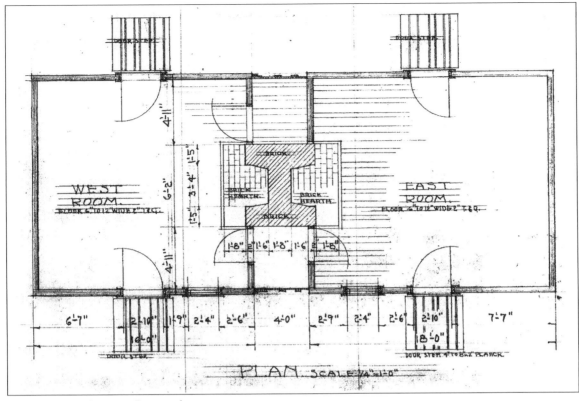

Floor plan of the Goosenest Prairie cabin.
From *An Archaeological and Architectural Assessment of the Lincoln Log Cabin*, Rural Macon County, Illinois.

The replica cabin constructed at The Lincoln Log Cabin State Historic Site. The site is an eighty-six-acre living-history park located eight miles south of Charleston, Illinois, near the town of Lerna. After Thomas Lincoln died in 1851, Abraham Lincoln owned and maintained the farm for his stepmother, Sarah Bush Lincoln. The site is operated by the Illinois Historic Preservation Agency.

Shiloh Cemetery, Charleston, Illinois

The historic cemetery adjoining the Shiloh Baptist Church near Charleston, Illinois, contains the graves of several Lincoln family members including Thomas Lincoln (1778-1851) and Sarah Bush Johnston Lincoln (1788-1869). **Above left:** View of Thomas Lincoln's grave with modern stone. Thomas Lincoln's grave was originally unmarked. Years later an obelisk-shaped stone **(Above right)** was placed on the grave. Still later, a modern granite stone **(Below right)** containing both Thomas Lincoln and Sarah Bush Lincoln's names replaced the earlier obelisk stone, which was moved a short distance away. **Below left:** The tombstone marking the grave of Lincoln's step-sister, Matilda Johnston Hall and her husband Squire Hall.

"Standing Tall." Sixty-two foot statue near Charleston, Illinois. Created in 1968 to commemorate the Lincoln Douglas Debates.

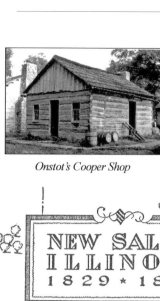
Onstot's Cooper Shop

Dr. Francis Renier House

Second Lincoln-Berry Store

Miller-Kelso House

NEW SALEM
ILLINOIS
1829 ★ 1839

Legend

1 HENRY ONSTOT'S CABIN
2 ONSTOT'S COOPER SHOP
3 TRENT BROTHER'S CABIN
4 MILLER-KELSO HOUSE
5 MILLER'S BLACKSMITH SHOP
6 ROBERT JOHNSON'S CABIN
7 ISAAC GOLLIHER'S CABIN
8 MARTIN WADDELL'S CABIN
9 ISAAC BURNER'S CABIN
10 HILL'S CARDING MILL
11 DR. FRANCIS REGNIER'S CABIN
12 SAMUEL HILL'S HOUSE
13 HILL-McNAMAR STORE
14 SECOND LINCOLN-BERRY STORE
15 FIRST LINCOLN-BERRY STORE
16 PETER LUKIN'S CABIN
17 DR. JOHN ALLEN'S CABIN
18 THE RUTLEDGE TAVERN
19 ROWAN HERNDON'S CABIN
20 DENTON OFFUT'S STORE
21 THE CLARY GROCERY
22 SAW AND GRIST MILL
23 SCHOOL AND CHURCH
24 THE OLD CEMETERY

ROMA DE PROCTOR DEL.

Louis A. Warren Library and Museum

Mentor Graham's School

Samuel Hill House

First Lincoln-Berry Store

Rutledge Tavern

New Salem being reconstructed in 1922.

New Salem
Lincoln's Alma Mater, 1831-1837

*He was a piece of floating driftwood, ... he had come
down the river with the freshet, borne along by the
swelling waters, and aimlessly floating about,
he had accidently lodged at New Salem.*   Abraham Lincoln

In many ways Abraham Lincoln was a late bloomer in life. While many of the traits that attracted people to Lincoln were always a part of his makeup, they emerged slowly over the first three decades of his life. And while many of these traits appear innate to his character, it took both time and environment to bring them to full expression. Always recognized as a "good fellow" with a keen sense of humor, it wasn't until his mid-twenties that people began to recognize something special in their strange friend. The village of New Salem and its people were the catalyst that stirred Lincoln and brought out the dormant qualities of his character and started him on the long road to becoming America's greatest leader.

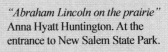

"Abraham Lincoln on the prairie"
Anna Hyatt Huntington. At the
entrance to New Salem State Park.

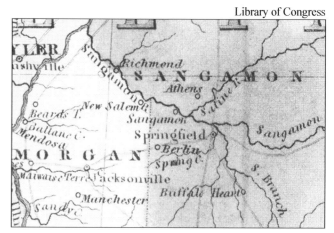

Lincoln's first visit to New Salem was more by accident than design. Following the winter of the "deep snow" of 1831, the now twenty-two year old Lincoln was ready to strike out on his own. The opportunity came through his cousin John Hanks. Hanks had contracted with a Springfield merchant and "big thinker" by the name of Denton Offut to take a shipment of goods down the Mississippi River to New Orleans to sell or swap for Louisiana goods. Offut was a complex man in many ways. An entrepreneur, he had a propensity for alcohol and could often be found in a local saloon drinking. He was a go-getter often stalled by drink. Hanks said that if Lincoln and his stepbrother John D. Johnston were interested in making the trip, he would

square it with Offut. The deal was struck and the three men set out to meet Offut near the town of Springfield where he would have a boat and cargo ready to sail.

When the three men arrived at the agreed upon site, Offut was nowhere to be found. Hanks, suspecting that Offut was probably living up to his reputation of a fondness for alcohol, found him drunk at the Buckhorn Tavern in Springfield. He had his cargo ready to ship, but no boat. The three men renegotiated the deal with an embarrassed Offut and set about building a flatboat.

In April, the boat was launched and the four men and their cargo headed down the Sangamon toward the Mississippi River. Arriving opposite the village of New Salem the flatboat became caught on the mill dam such that the bow was suspended over the dam in mid-air while the stern, loaded with cargo, slowly began taking on water. The boat, with all its cargo, was in danger of sinking. People from the village began to gather along the shore, watching as the boat continued to take on water. Lincoln quickly took charge of the situation and, commandeering a second flatboat, had some of the cargo transferred to the other boat. Having lightened

Modern example of the type of flatboat built to transport Denton Offut's cargo to New Orleans. Eighty-foot long and eighteen-foot wide, the boat was later referred to as "Offut's Ark." It took six weeks to build from harvesting trees to the finished product. The men were paid by Offut twelve dollars a month to build the boat from scratch.

Reconstructed grist and saw mill established in 1829 by James Rutledge and John Cameron on the Sangamon River at New Salem.

the flatboat's load, Lincoln waded ashore where he borrowed an augur. Returning to the boat, he proceeded to drill a hole in the floor of the suspended bow letting the water drain out. When water had finished draining, Lincoln hammered a plug into the hole and the boat slid over the dam, free to continue its journey. The crowd gathered on shore, impressed by Lincoln's ingenuity, cheered as he waded ashore to return the borrowed augur. It was a simple solution but one that drew the admiration of the residents of the village. Lincoln, they said, was quite a clever fellow. Denton Offut agreed. He knew he had found just the man to run his business. New Salem, Lincoln thought, was just the place where he might settle down to begin his new life away from home and on his own.

The Rutledge Tavern where Lincoln boarded on his arrival to the village before moving into Offut's store.

Lincoln and New Salem were a perfect match. Again, Offut agreed. He thought the village an ideal place for his new store and Lincoln just the man to run it. Offut was always looking for new opportunities and told Lincoln he would open a store in New Salem when they returned from New Orleans. Lincoln, Offut said, could be his clerk if he wanted. Lincoln readily agreed and following the trip to New Orleans headed for New Salem to await Offutt's return with a cargo of new supplies. Clerking appealed to Lincoln. It was a good occupation for starters and someday he might even own his own store. New Salem, he thought, was a perfect place for a young man with ambition to start his new life.

The village of New Salem was located twenty miles to the northwest of Springfield and situated on a bluff overlooking the Sangamon River. For two hundred and fifty miles the river courses its way through central Illinois before emptying into the Illinois River on its way to the Mississippi. One of its claims to fame is its association with Abraham Lincoln and the village of New Salem, which the river passes on its way to joining the Illinois River at Beardstown.

New Salem was founded in 1829 by James Rutledge and John Cameron, two entrepreneurs who built a mill on the banks of the famous river and purchased the bluff just to the west of the mill. They proceeded to lay off fifty-two lots that the two men sold for between seven dollars and fifty cents and twelve dollars. By the summer of 1831, the village had grown to twenty-five buildings arranged along a dirt road that ran toward the river before veering to the north, running through a grove of trees past a saloon owned by a man named William Clary.

The village soon filled with merchants and artisans including a cooper, a blacksmith, a cobbler, a general store, a carding mill, a doctor, and a tavern or inn. A total of twenty-five families inhabited the village at its peak, its population around one hundred people. By contrast, the city of Springfield had a population of eight hundred people. But while the town of Springfield rapidly grew into a city, the village of New Salem slowly declined until it was abandoned by 1839, two years after Lincoln moved to Springfield.

New Salem has been referred to as Lincoln's "alma

The Sangamon River as seen from the bluff overlooking the river at New Salem.

mater." No period of time before or after Lincoln's six years in the Illinois village were more important to the nurture of his character or to the launching of his career. It is hard to imagine Lincoln successfully acquiring the self-confidence or gaining the loyal patronage of so many people in any setting other than that of a pioneer community of close knit and self-reliant people as he came into contact with in New Salem. It was in New Salem that Lincoln evolved from a "piece of floating driftwood," as he referred to himself, into a self-reliant man with a purpose.

New Salem broadened his education, gave him gainful employment, and launched his political career that led to his introduction to the law and influential friends. His six-year course of "study" served as both an academic enlightenment and a school of hard knocks. As he matured in stature he strengthened in resolve. During his tenure he served in the state militia, went to war, buried his dead comrades, clerked in a store, was part owner of two stores, lost everything in bankruptcy, was appointed postmaster, worked as a surveyor, was twice elected to the state legislature (after being defeated), studied law,

"Uncle Jimmy" Short

was admitted to the bar, suffered an unfulfilled love affair through tragic death, and was rejected in a proposal for marriage. By the time he had decided to leave the small community of friends, he was fully prepared to take his case to a higher court. Still unsure of himself in some ways, he needed only to test the course to find that he was not lacking.

New Salem's interesting array of people exposed Lincoln to newer and better ways. Here he developed his skills of both writing and public speaking with the help of a teacher and a debater. He was introduced to the majesty of William Shakespeare and Robert Burns. He learned to calculate both numbers and people, and was shown unselfish charity by a neighbor who respected him for his future as well as his past. Failing in business, Lincoln was forced to surrender the instruments of his newly learned means of support, surveying, to a sheriff's auction to satisfy the debts he incurred while operating a store. Even his horse was taken from him leaving him little hope of securing even a modest livelihood. Unbeknownst to Lincoln, a neighbor, "Uncle Jimmy" Short, successfully bid on the horse and surveying instruments only to give them back to Lincoln as a symbol of faith in Lincoln's worthiness (Lincoln eventually paid back the money to Short).

Having known sorrow and pain only too well, Lincoln had also known failure. Now he learned just how good-hearted a fellow human being could be in Short's act of kindness. With the good wishes of such people, Lincoln was sure to succeed eventually, and succeed he would.

The spring following his arrival in New Salem saw Indian incursions into the white man's settlements. The great Sauk chief, Black Hawk, had rallied his people and, breaking an agreement, crossed the Mississippi River to reclaim lands once belonging to his people. A call went out for a gathering of the state militia and Lincoln, along with several of his New Salem neighbors, signed up.

New Salem at sunrise.

The Rutledge Family and Their Tavern

James and Mary Ann Rutledge had nine children during the time they lived in New Salem. Among the nine were Ann Rutledge, Lincoln's alleged sweetheart, and David Rutledge who served with Lincoln in the Black Hawk War. In May of 1833, James Rutledge moved his family to Sandridge, a community located several miles north of New Salem. It was at Sandridge that Ann Rutledge succumbed to typhoid fever in 1835.

From a postcard, ca. 1950.

Scene inside Rutledge Tavern.

A Famous Wrestling Match Wins the Day for Lincoln

In August, two months after Lincoln arrived in New Salem, Denton Offut opened his store and hired Lincoln as a clerk. The store was within a stone's throw of William Clary's grocery (saloon) where a group of "toughs" known as the Clary's Grove boys frequently hung out. Led by their leader Jack Armstrong, the boys were well-known for their rowdy behavior. Fights were common and most villagers looked on the gang as a bunch of bullies. Offut wasted no time bragging about Lincoln's athletic abilities, chiding the Clary's Grove boys that Lincoln could whip any one of them in a match. Armstrong couldn't let Offut's chiding pass and challenged Lincoln to a wrestling match. A time and place was set and word spread quickly through the village.

What happened is still a matter of conjecture. Some accounts have Lincoln besting Armstrong. Others have the pair stalemated until Armstrong broke the rules by grabbing Lincoln's leg and throwing him. Other stories have Armstrong's gang of roughs trying to intervene when their leader looked like he was about to lose. But whether Lincoln threw Armstrong or Armstrong unfairly tripped Lincoln, the match passed into the upper ranks of American folklore. The incident sealed Lincoln's reputation as a formidable member of the community. He and Armstrong became fast friends. It gave Lincoln "standing" with both the Clary's Grove boys and the villagers who had little use for Armstrong and his "toughs."

Lincoln later became a good friend of Hannah Armstrong, Jack's wife. Years later when the match was only a dim memory, Lincoln successfully defended Hannah's son, Duff Armstrong, against a murder charge in the famous "Almanac" trial. Lincoln came to Hannah's aid again in 1863 when he ordered the discharge of her boy from the army so he could go home and take care of his mother.

Over the years the wrestling match grew into a legend of major proportions. It was the stuff of movies and comic books as seen in the accompanying illustration that appeared as the cover of a 1958 *Classics Illustrated*, a comic book devoted to portraying great events and people in history.

Uncle Jimmy Short described Lincoln as a scientific wrestler, which merely meant that Lincoln wrestled according to prescribed rules as opposed to a free-for-all style.

Hannah Armstrong said in an interview with William Herndon in 1866: "A few days before Mr. Lincoln left for Washington I went to see him – was a widow – the boys got up a story on me that I went to get to sleep with Abe etc. – I replied to the joke that it was not every woman who had the good fortune & high honor of sleeping with a President. This stopped the sport – cut it short."

In describing Lincoln, Hannah Armstrong told Herndon: "Abe would come out to our house – drink milk & mush – corn bread and butter – bring the children candy – would rock the cradle of my baby. Jack Armstrong and Lincoln never had a bad word – they did wrestle – no foul play – all in good humor – commenced in fun and ended in sport."

Opposite page: Classics Illustrated, *No. 142 Gilberton Company, Inc. (1958) (Author's Collection.)*

Jack Armstrong
Abraham Lincoln Presidential Library and Museum

Hannah Armstrong (Photo taken later in life.)
Abraham Lincoln Presidential Library and Museum

Clary's Grove

Clary's Grove was settled by John Clary, a Tennessean who immigrated to the area in 1819. He was soon followed by other members of the Clary clan, creating a small settlement appended to the growing village of New Salem. The first house to have glass windows instead of greased paper was built by George Spears in Clary's Grove in 1830.

John Clary's brother, William Clary, founded Clary's Grocery located on the bluff overlooking the gristmill. "Grocery" was the word used for saloon in the early pioneer days, and Clary's grocery quickly became the favorite gathering place for the local "roughnecks" who spent much of their time drinking and fighting. Historian Benjamin Thomas described the "Clary's Grove boys" as "a reckless, roistering, fearless crowd." While rough, even cruel at times, "they were also generous and sympathetic." Any stranger who came to town had to sooner or later deal with the Clary's Grove boys or be shamed. Challenges were a regular part of the neighborhood's weekly doings.

Principal among the Clary's Grove boys was Jack Armstrong, the big buck of the lick. Armstrong earned his place at the head of the pack by besting every man that was foolish enough to take him on. Denton Offutt, Lincoln's first benefactor and employer in New Salem, bragged openly that his man Abe could "out-run, out-throw, and whip any man in the village, bar none." Offutt's brag delighted the Clary's Grove boys, and a challenge was arranged between their champion, Jack Armstrong, and Lincoln. The match took place, and while several versions have passed

down through folklore, the end result was the acceptance of Lincoln by the rough gang and the life-long friendship between Lincoln and Armstrong. In 1857, Lincoln the lawyer would successfully defend the widow Hannah Armstrong's son Duff from a murder charge.

In the spring of 1832 when the governor of Illinois called for volunteers from the state militia to put down the incursion into Illinois by the Fox chief Black Hawk, Lincoln along with several of the Clary's Grove boys enlisted for thirty day's service. As was the custom in those days, the men in the ranks elected their own officers. With the unanimous support of the Clary's Grove boys, Lincoln was elected captain by an overwhelming majority. One officer from another company remarked that Lincoln's men, as they were now called, were, "the hardest set of men he ever saw." Lincoln, it was said, was the only man who held the respect of the crew of rough frontiersmen.

In 1833, the Clary's Grove boys broke into the store of Reuben Radford, breaking windows and destroying part of his inventory. The reason remains a mystery, but Radford had had enough and sold out his entire stock to William Greene who, in turn, sold it to Lincoln and William Berry, giving rise to the Lincoln-Berry store.

Like most of New Salem, Clary's Grove slowly faded away as family after family moved north to Sandridge and Petersburg. In 1839, the state legislature established Petersburg as the county seat, signaling the death knell for New Salem. By 1840, it and Clary's Grove passed into history.

Store of Samuel Hill. Lincoln is believed to have served as postmaster of New Salem in this store.

Gentleman docent resting on the porch of a New Salem cabin.

Lady docents quilting on a lazy summer day.

Top left: *Joshua Miller-Jack Kelso cabin. The Miller-Kelso cabin was one of the first buildings to be constructed in the village. It consists of two large rooms separated by a "dog trot." Lincoln visited both families on numerous occasions, often taking his meals with the Millers and Kelsos.*

Top right: *Joshua Miller. Miller and his wife lived in one half of the double cabin next to Miller's blacksmith shop. Jack Kelso and his wife Hannah lived in the other half. Kelso was a lover of books and poetry, a love that resulted in a strong bond with Lincoln. From a carte de visite in the Fern Nance Pond Collection.*

Left: *Trent brothers cabin. Alexander and Martin Trent bought out Lincoln and Berry's store only to see it fail under their management along with the rest of New Salem.*

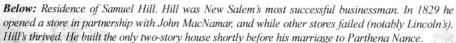

Below: *Residence of Samuel Hill. Hill was New Salem's most successful businessman. In 1829 he opened a store in partnership with John MacNamar, and while other stores failed (notably Lincoln's), Hill's thrived. He built the only two-story house shortly before his marriage to Parthena Nance.*

Left: Henry and Susan Onstot. Onstot came to New Salem in 1830 and established a cooperage. In 1834 he purchased the Rutledge Tavern and after a year resold it, using the money to build a new residence and cooper shop. Abraham Lincoln Presidential Library and Museum.

Below: Onstot cooperage. Onstot's trade as a barrel maker made him one of the more prosperous merchants in New Salem. His house, built in 1835 with the money from the sale of the Rutledge Tavern, was made of the finest materials and craftsmanship. It had wooden floors of sawn boards, and all of the latches were made of iron. He moved his cooper shop to Petersburg when he and his wife left New Salem. The building was rescued in 1923 and returned to the reconstructed village as one of the original buildings.

Lincoln Keeps Store

Right: *Denton Offutt's store where Lincoln first clerked after coming to live in New Salem in July 1831.*

Center: *First Berry-Lincoln store purchased from the Herndon brothers in the summer of 1832.*

Below: *New Salem's only sheathed building. William Berry and Lincoln opened their second store in this building purchased from Reuben Radford in 1833 after the Clary's Grove boys vandalized the store and its inventory. Lincoln sold his interest to Berry a few months later, apparently due to Berry's alcohol problems and Lincoln's mounting debt. On May 7, 1833, Lincoln was appointed postmaster at New Salem and had his office in Samuel Hill's store.*

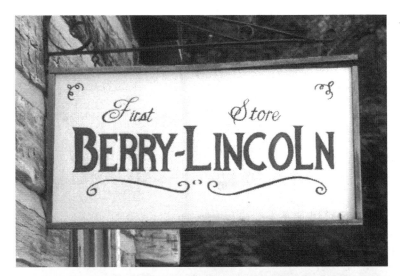

Left: Modern sign on the first Berry-Lincoln store.

Center: Lincoln's alleged bed displayed in the rear shed of the second Berry-Lincoln store.

Below: Denton Offut's store in the recreated village of New Salem. The photograph was taken by a member of the "Black Hawk Hiking Club" at the time of their "Big Hike" to the newly reconstructed village of New Salem in 1922. From the collection of Edward Steers, Jr.

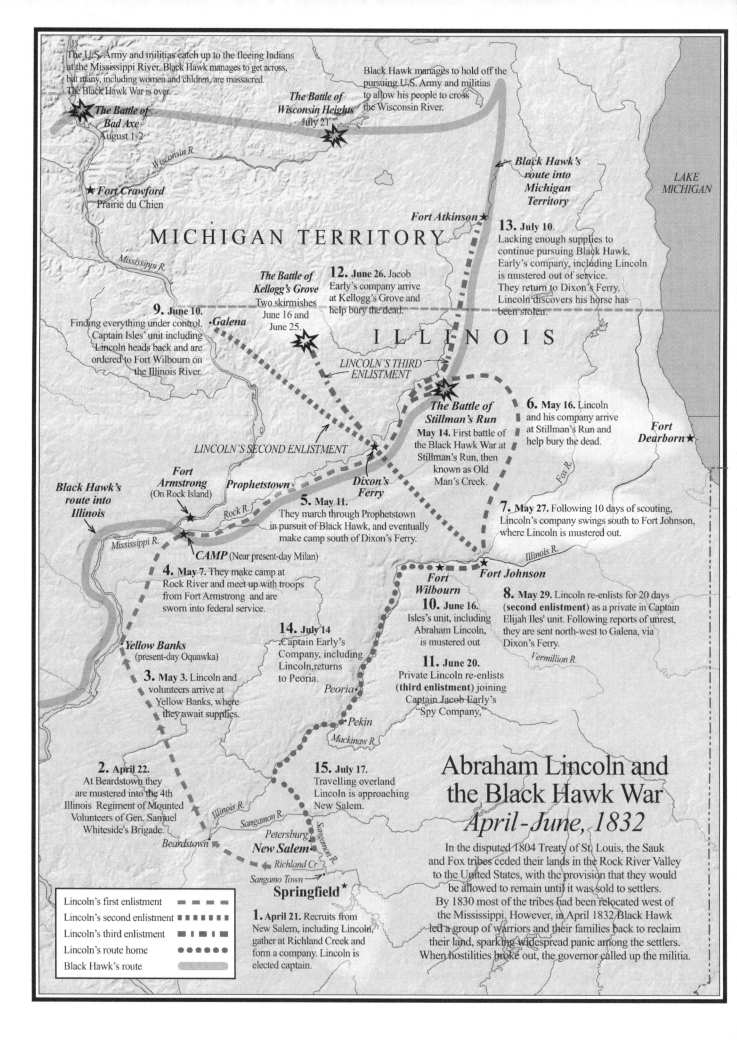

Lincoln and the Black Hawk War

In the spring of 1832, nine months after Lincoln arrived in New Salem, a rider galloped into the small village with a message from the governor. Black Hawk, the great chief of the Sauk nation, had led a large contingent of Indians east across the Mississippi River back into Illinois. The migrating party included 1,500 women, children, and older men, in addition to 500 warriors. It was not a typical war party but a migration back to their traditional land that they had been forced to leave a year before. The Sauk leaders had signed a treaty on June 30, 1831, known as "The Articles of Agreement and Capitulation." The treaty ordered the Sauk to cross the Mississippi River into Iowa and never return to their former lands without permission from the governor of Illinois or the President of the United States. For agreeing, Black Hawk and his people received sixty thousand bushels of corn.

During the War of 1812 the Sauk had sided with the British and fought against the Americans. The British, Black Hawk said, at least kept their word to the Indian while the American's word was not to be trusted. When the British gave up and returned home for the second time in two wars with the Americans, Black Hawk and his people returned to the treaty of 1804 banning them east of the Mississippi. Now the white man broke his word again and began selling land that the Indian hunted and lived on. Black Hawk believed that land could not be sold. Only those things that could be carried off could be sold. The land was given by Man-ee-do, the Great Spirit, and was for people to fish and hunt on, but no man owned. The great Sauk and Fox nations had enough of the white man's lies and now returned to their ancestral grounds and old village of Saukenuk where the Rock River entered the Mississippi.

Alarmed by the migration of such a large contingent of Indians into Illinois, governor John Reynolds called for all patriot men to come forward and defend their land against the Indian invader. Illinois law required all white males between the ages of eighteen and forty-five to serve in the state militia. Lincoln, along with the young men of New Salem, volunteered

Captain Lincoln
by Leonard Crunelle, Dixon, Illinois.

for thirty days service. In all, sixty-seven men from around the county had stepped forward, forming a company of militia. As was customary at the time, the men chose their own officers. To Lincoln's great surprise, over two-thirds of the men voted for Lincoln, electing him captain of their small company. Many years later Lincoln would write that his election by his comrades "was a success which gave me more pleasure than any I have had since."

Lincoln served three tours or enlistments in the militia totalling ninety days of service in all. During all three enlistments he never saw action, although he experienced virtually every other aspect of such a military campaign. He experienced privation when rations ran out at one point, was arrested twice for offences not uncommon among militia, and, as commanding officer of a company, experienced insubordination that could only be handled by personally threatening physical force, and was part of a burial detail that had to bury the losers in a recent battle with Black Hawk's warriors.

Frontier militia were a rough lot at best and, unlike the discipline of the regular army, practiced a form of democracy that ran counter to successful military protocol. William Cullen Bryant, then editor of the *New York Post*, on visiting the area described the militia of which Lincoln was a part: "They were a hard-looking set of men, unkempt and unshaven, wearing shirts of dark calico, and sometimes calico compotes, ...some of the settlers complained that they made war upon the pigs and chickens." Bryant, having actually met Lincoln, described him "a raw youth, in whose quaint and pleasant talk he was interested."

At Beardstown Lincoln was challenged by a member of another company to a wrestling match and for the first time in his frontier career was thrown by his opponent. Lincoln came back to throw his adversary the next two times and won the match to remain the undefeated champion of wrestling matches. He was arrested and had to surrender his sword for a day, a symbol of authority and rank, after discharging his rifle in camp, a violation of military regulations. Later he was arrested a second time after some of the men under his command broke into and stole several bottles of whiskey from the officers' supply. The men became so drunk that they were unfit for duty and could not march the next day. Lincoln was sentenced to carry a wooden sword for two days, symbolic of his failure to control his rough recruits.

Another test of Lincoln's command came one evening when Patawatomi, an elderly Indian wandered into camp. Set upon by the band of militia, the Indian produced a letter from the commanding general stating that he was a friendly Indian who had helped the settlers and was to be treated as an ally. The militiamen, who still had not fought a single Indian, declared their intention of killing the old warrior. Lincoln stepped in and told his men to back off and respect the old Indian's letter. When called a coward

Lincoln protecting Patawatomi.
Wikimedia Commons

Chief Black Hawk by Lorado Taft.
GNU Free Documentation License,
Free Software Foundation.

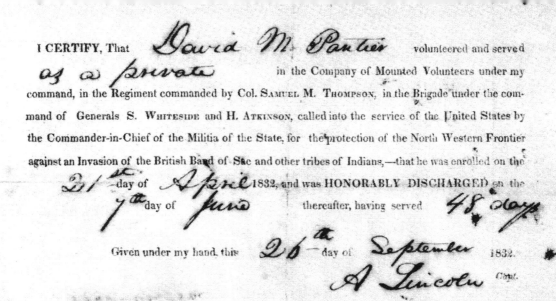

I CERTIFY, That *David M. Pantier* volunteered and served *as a private* in the Company of Mounted Volunteers under my command, in the Regiment commanded by Col. SAMUEL M. THOMPSON, in the Brigade under the command of Generals S. WHITESIDE and H. ATKINSON, called into the service of the United States by the Commander-in-Chief of the Militia of the State, for the protection of the North Western Frontier against an Invasion of the British Band of Sac and other tribes of Indians,—that he was enrolled on the *21st* day of *April* 1832, and was HONORABLY DISCHARGED on the *7th* day of *June* thereafter, having served *48 days*

Given under my hand, this *26th* day of *September* 1832.

A Lincoln Capt.

by some of the men, Lincoln challenged each man, stating they would have to test his courage first before dealing with the Indian. The men wisely backed off and left both Lincoln and the Indian alone.

Serving among the American forces during the short campaign were several Americans whose paths would cross with Lincoln in the distant future. When he reenlisted for his second tour, Lincoln was mustered into service by Second Lieutenant Robert Anderson of the 3rd U.S. Artillery. Serving in various positions with the militia were Zachary Taylor, Albert Sidney Johnston, Jefferson Davis, Edward D. Baker, and John T. Stuart.

Lincoln was mustered out of service on July 10, 1832, and began the long trip home to New Salem, made especially difficult because his horse, and that of his friend George Harrison, had been stolen the night before. The two men canoed down the Illinois River to the small village of Havana where they sold their canoe and continued their journey on foot, arriving at the end of the month. Back in Wisconsin, the defeat of Black Hawk at the battle of Bad Axe brought an end to hostilities. The Indians were forced into signing a new treaty that now annexed a large share of their lands west of the Mississippi.

Lincoln and his company had become part of a burial detail. On June 26, 1832, following the battle of Kellogg's Grove, they approached the battleground. Lincoln described the scene: "I remember just how those men looked ... the red light of the morning sun was streaming upon them as they lay heads towards us on the ground ... every man had a round, red spot on top of his head, about as big as a dollar where the redskins had taken his scalp. It was frightful, but it was grotesque, and the red sunlight seemed to pain everything all over. I remember that one man had buckskin breeches on."

Chief Blackhawk
by Homer Henderson, 1837.

Depiction of the Indian Crees Massacre that started the Black Hawk War.

Serving in various positions with the Militia during the Black Hawk War were Zachary Taylor, Albert Sidney Johnston, Jefferson Davis, Edward D. Baker, and John T. Stuart. Photos from Library of Congress

The war memorial for the Battle of Stillman's Run, the first battle of the Black Hawk War of 1832, is located near Stillman Valley, Illinois. Dr. Gordon E. Dammann.

28

The Battle of Kellogg's Grove

Nine days after the skirmish between Illinois militia and warriors of the Saux and Fox nation led by Black Hawk, five militiamen were killed. Left on the field by the retreating militia, the dead men were scalped by Black Hawk's warriors. Abraham Lincoln arrived at the scene as part of a relief attachment, and helped bury the dead along with several dead militiamen from an earlier battle. Years later Lincoln commented on his experience:

The battle site consists of a one-and-a-half-acre park placed on the United States National Register of Historic Places in 1978. The cemetery contains the remains of the eleven militiamen killed during the two skirmishes at the site.

Right: Battle Monument and Cemetery at Kellogg's Grove. Erected in 1887, the 34-foot monument is topped with a pyramid of cannonballs. Eighteen graves lie at the base, the whole enclosed by an iron fence.
Dr. Gordon E. Dammann.

Below: Grave markers of the eighteen militiamen buried at the base of the monument at Kellogg's Grove.
Dr. Gordon E. Dammann.

LINCOLN
AND ANN RUTLEDGE
AND THE PIONEERS OF NEW SALEM
A Lecture by
WILLIAM H. HERNDON

Introduction by
Harry Rosecrans Burke

19   45

TROVILLION PRIVATE PRESS
at the sign of the silver horse
HERRIN, ILLINOIS

He Loves Me,
He Loves Me Not
Abe and Ann Rutledge

*I cannot endure the thought that sleet
and storm, frost and snow of heaven should
beat on her grave.*

A. Lincoln *(maybe)*

The Lincoln landscape is littered with mythology, folklore, and outright fraud. Determining fact from fiction can be among the more frustrating aspects of writing, but, then again, can be among the more enjoyable to the intrepid researcher. The alleged romance between Abraham Lincoln and Ann Rutledge is one of those events that inspire both poet and cynic alike. Whether fact or fiction, the alleged love affair between Abe and Ann has warmed the hearts of millions. The story of their romance first came to light in a minor article in the *Menard Axis* in 1862. The article was written by the paper's editor, John Hill, a son of Samuel Hill who was a highly successful merchant in New Salem and who once attempted to court Ann Rutledge. In the article, Hill briefly mentions an ill-fated romance between the aspiring Lincoln and an unnamed woman who possessed charms. The article passed unnoticed until 1866 when William Herndon set out to detail Lincoln's New Salem life a year after his death and some thirty-one years after the love affair allegedly took place.

Herndon, Lincoln's law partner and biographer, after much correspondence with Lincoln's New Salem neighbors set out to tell the world about Ann Rutledge in an 1866 lecture delivered in Lincoln's hometown of Springfield. The lecture, a rambling description of the village of New Salem and the surrounding landscape ended with the story of the love affair between the two star-crossed lovers during the early 1830s. Herndon told his audience that "Lincoln loved Ann Rutledge better than his own life." Importantly, Ann's tragic death in 1835 saved Lincoln for his true destiny of saving the Union and freeing the slaves. For, if Ann and Abe had married, he would have settled down to a blissful life, content with a loving wife and children.

When Lincoln arrived in the village of New Salem in July 1831, he was twenty-two years old and had had no serious affair with any woman. By his own words, he was shy to the point of being introverted. "A woman," he wrote, "is the only thing I am afraid of that I know will not hurt me."

From a postcard, ca. 1950.
H.N. Shonkwiler,
Springfield, IL.

But then, he had almost no opportunity to interact with women his own age during the early years of his life. Life on the Indiana frontier during Lincoln's growing years (1816-1830) presented little opportunity for young romance. New Salem presented the first serious opportunity in the form of Ann Rutledge, an attractive nineteen-year-old girl who, according to Hill and others, was a young woman who was "lovely, angelic, and the height of perfection," characteristics Lincoln was definitely attracted to.

William Herndon
Library of Congress

Ann was born January 10, 1813, in Kentucky, the third of ten children born to Mary and James Rutledge. She was described by her older sister as quite pretty with dark blue eyes, sandy hair, and a fair complexion. She stood five feet two inches tall, weighing around one hundred and twenty pounds and, although lacking formal education, was considered quite intelligent. Her father founded the village of New Salem along with his partner John Cameron in 1829 when Ann was sixteen years old.

On Lincoln's arrival in New Salem in 1831, two years after its founding, the village consisted of some twenty-five families comprising a population of over one hundred and fifty people. Pickings were slim among the small population and it seemed only natural that Lincoln would be attracted to someone like Ann Rutledge despite his shyness. Unfortunately, Ann, now eighteen, was already betrothed to a successful businessman in the village by the name of John McNamar. McNamar was part owner along with Samuel Hill of a

large, successful store in the village.

McNamar was something of an enigma. His real name was John McNeil. McNeil, originally from Ohio County, New York, later claimed to have changed his name to McNamar to avoid being traced by his parents. He wanted to strike out on his own and after achieving financial success, return to New York and pay off his father's numerous debts. Arriving in New Salem, McNamar (McNeil) achieved financial success and along the way fell in love with the village beauty, Ann Rutledge. By all descriptions, Ann was a lovely girl with a loving character. She was a dream come true for any young man who found himself in her presence.

McNamar proposed marriage to Ann and she accepted. But McNamar was still encumbered with freeing his father from heavy debt. And so, in July 1832 (exactly one year after Lincoln's arrival), McNamar told Ann he had to return to New York and settle his father's affairs. Once he had accomplished his task he would return and the two would be married. It was at this time that he presumably told Ann his real name was McNeil and the reason for assuming an alias. Ann agreed to wait for her fiancé's return, assuming it would be a matter of months. Unfortunately for Ann, months turned into years; three to be exact. McNamar left for New York in the fall of 1832 and did not return until September 1835, two weeks after Ann's death on August 25, 1835. He had been absent for just over three years. He wrote to Ann sparingly during the first year of his absence until the final two years when all communication ceased. Ann was left to wonder if her engagement was still in effect, binding her to a man who might never return. Enter Abraham Lincoln.

Lincoln arrived in New Salem in July 1831 at a time when Ann and John McNamar were lovers and engaged to be married. After McNamar's departure, Lincoln and Ann became good friends. Their minds tended to run along the same channels and the two enjoyed many of the same things. Ann was eager to learn and Lincoln was eager to teach. Among the few precious relics from this period is a copy of Kirkham's English Grammar with an inscription (not in Lincoln's hand) that reads, "Ann

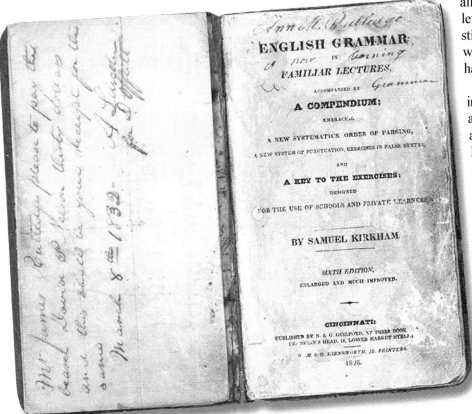

Kirkham's English Grammar
Library of Congress

M. Rutledge is now learning grammar." Did the two study grammar together? And if they did, does it mean they were lovers or simply sharing a common interest in learning? At this point the story runs off in two divergent directions, both firmly entrenched in the minds of those who love Lincoln and those who study Lincoln. The first of these stories is that of a platonic friendship, nothing more. The second involves passionate love leading to an engagement – the first for Lincoln, the second for Ann.

In the love version of our story, it was during McNamar's prolonged absence of nearly three years that the two friends slowly fell in love, leading to Ann's agreement to marry Lincoln. Seemingly engaged to two men, Ann told Lincoln he must wait until she could obtain a release from her engagement to the absent John McNamar. Tragedy struck when in August 1835, with McNamar still missing and Ann and Lincoln deeply in love, Ann became ill with typhoid fever. After several days of fever and retching, Ann died.

The story continues of a distraught Lincoln so devastated by Ann's death that he frightened his friends and neighbors by appearing to be on the brink of suicide. Tales go so far as to describe Lincoln spending hours at Ann's graveside, throwing himself over the freshly dug sod to protect her from the harsh elements as she slept the peaceful sleep of the dead. Weeks would pass before Lincoln began to regain his reason and relieve his friends

Joanne Woodward portraying Ann Rutledge in the 1952 Omnibus *series,* "Mr. Lincoln," *written by James Agee.* RSA Venture LLC.

of their worry that he had lost his mind. Unable to work or function without the close supervision of friends, Lincoln slowly accepted Ann's death as yet another test "in this sad world of ours." Ann was the third woman, after his mother and older sister, to die unexpectedly, leaving him despondent.

The jury of academic historians remains split on the question of a love affair between the two with the majority of historians believing the story while a minor group considering the story pure myth dredged up by William Herndon and promulgated by Hollywood and television's desire to tell a good story. Both sides have marshaled evidence to support their position. The general public, however, has little doubt of the love affair's authenticity. It is a remarkably touching story, one that is easy to believe.

Like Lincoln's assassination in 1865, Ann's death in 1835 at the tender age of twenty-two became the stuff of legend. And like Lincoln's assassination, the alleged affair didn't take flight until several years after the fact. It's birth occurred on November 16, 1866, in Springfield, Illinois, and William Herndon served as its midwife. On that evening, Herndon addressed a small crowd of Lincoln's neighbors in Springfield's Practical Business College. His lecture, titled *Abraham Lincoln, Miss Ann Rutledge, New Salem, Pioneering, and the Poem,* set off a firestorm as Lincoln lovers everywhere viewed Hern-

Henry Fonda portraying Abraham Lincoln in the 20th Century Fox production, "Young Mr. Lincoln." 20th Century Fox.

don's claim that Ann was Lincoln's first and only love as "an insidious attack on the holy estate of matrimony." More specifically, it was viewed as a direct attack against Lincoln's wife, Mary Todd Lincoln. It was widely known that the two held a deep hatred of one another. Although Lincoln's law partner for twenty-one years, Herndon was forbidden by Mary Lincoln to set foot in the Lincoln home. Herndon's view of Mary Lincoln, and her marriage, was equally hateful. William E. Barton, one of the early biographers of Lincoln and an indefatigable researcher, branded Herndon's story, "a wicked stab into the broken heart" of Mary Lincoln. Lincoln's closest friends agreed.

Following Lincoln's death, Herndon set out to gather as much information as he could about his famous law partner. It rapidly became his passion. He began by writing to numerous former acquaintances and neighbors of Lincoln during his New Salem period. It was at this time that Herndon first learned of an alleged affair between Lincoln and Rutledge. It didn't take Herndon long before he concluded an affair existed, and that it involved an engagement to marry. Despite his long friendship with Lincoln, it was the first time Herndon heard of any love affair in his partner's early life other than that with Mary Todd.

Mary Todd Lincoln
From a carte de visite

The first piece of evidence Herndon uncovered came from the Rutledge family and, in particular, Robert Rutledge, Ann's younger brother. Who better to know the circumstances of the relationship between Ann and Lincoln than Ann's own family? It was the Rutledge family who had a vested interest in associating their beloved Ann with the man the country came

to view as its savior and greatest statesman.

In response to Herndon's enquiries in the summer of 1866, Robert Rutledge, just seventeen at the time of Ann's death, wrote at great length describing Lincoln's New Salem years and the relationship between Ann and John McNamar. Robert's testimony included interviews with his mother, Mary Ann Rutledge and his brother John Rutledge, but strangely, not with any of his other Rutledge siblings. All of Robert's testimony to Herndon was hearsay. He told how McNamar left New Salem to return to New York to care for his ailing parents. In his prolonged absence, Ann and Lincoln slowly fell in love and agreed to marry once Ann confronted McNamar and received her release from their engagement. Tragedy would intervene when Ann took sick with typhoid and died leaving Lincoln in utter despair. Robert wrote, in part, "In August 1835 Ann sickened and died. The effect upon Mr. Lincoln's mind was terrible; he became plunged in despair, and many of his friends feared that reason would desert her throne. His extraordinary emotions were regarded as strong evidence of the existence of the tenderest relations between himself and the deceased."

The claim of Lincoln's strange behavior following Ann's death is often cited as proof of a love affair that went well beyond a platonic relationship by those who otherwise claimed no first-hand knowledge of an affair. Lincoln might grieve for a lost friend, but to lose control of his sanity and act so irrationally as to worry his closest friends that he might contemplate suicide surely goes beyond friendship. According to author John Evangelist Walsh in *The Shadows Rise. Abraham Lincoln and the Ann Rutledge Legend*, a parade of witnesses came forward to bolster Robert Rutledge's claim of a romantic relationship including betrothal. Unfortunately, most of the statements proved to provide little definitive and often conflicting information, and even doubt at times.

One of Lincoln's closest friends in New Salem was

Reconstructed Rutledge tavern in New Salem as it was in 1922.
Fern Nance Pond, New Salem Vilage, Forgotten Books, 1954.

"Uncle Jimmy" Short. Short was the man who purchased Lincoln's surveying equipment and horse during a sheriff's sale when Lincoln went bust and could not pay his debts. After Short purchased the items at auction he generously returned them to Lincoln so he could keep working as a surveyor, a generous act showing the great respect and love he had for Lincoln. Short had employed Mary Ann Rutledge, Ann's mother, as his housekeeper and was quite familiar with the Rutledge family. Short later wrote to Herndon that he "did not know of any engagement or tender passages between Mr. L and Miss R at the time. But after her death – he seemed to be so much affected and grieved so hardly that I then supposed there must have been something." Here again we see Lincoln's alleged behavior after Ann's death offered as proof that the two were in love and engaged to be married without ever having witnessed any signs of a romance between the two. And perhaps, equally significant, is John McNamar's response to Herndon's questions: "I had never heard that Mr. Lincoln addressed Miss Ann Rutledge in terms of courtship." Also telling is that Lincoln never spoke of Ann Rutledge during his lifetime except on one occasion, and that has come under question. Isaac Cogdal, a former resident of

"Uncle Jimmy" Short

New Salem who, like Lincoln, became a lawyer, visited Lincoln in Springfield in 1860 when Lincoln was president-elect. Years later he told of their conversation: "Abe is it true you fell in love with & courted Ann Rutledge?" Cogdal asked. According to Cogdal, Lincoln answered, "It is true – true indeed I did. I have loved the name Rutledge to this day." Cogdal pressed on, "Is it true you ran a little wild about the matter?" Lincoln answered, "I did really – I ran off the track: it was my first. I loved the woman dearly & sacredly … think often – often of her now."

While Lincoln was, as Herndon described him, "the most shut-mouthed man ever," the open confession to Cogdal seems quite out of character. Yet, Cogdal was from New Salem and had no reason to misrepresent Lincoln. Still, most historians dismiss Cogdal's reminiscences of a conversation with Lincoln years after it happened as fantasy.

Countering the claims by Robert Rutledge and others concerning Lincoln's running "off the track" is the case of William Marsh. Marsh, a resident of New Salem at the time of Ann's death, wrote a letter home to his brother three weeks after Ann died in which he describes Lincoln as "a very clever fellow." Marsh writes that he persuaded Lincoln to "free frank" a letter for him, which Lincoln did, a violation of the postal regulations. As postmaster,

Lincoln had the right to allow certain mail to be sent without the required postage. According to Marsh, Lincoln was his usual self. One week after the encounter at the post office Lincoln ran a survey on a ten acre lot for Marsh on a piece of property Marsh wanted to buy, an action that required considerable skill. At no time did Marsh mention any behavior of Lincoln's out of the ordinary. The ability to carry out an extensive survey at a time when Lincoln was said to be despondent and suicidal contradicts claims that Lincoln was too distraught to function.

It is also important to realize that thirteen months after Ann's death Lincoln set out to court another woman,

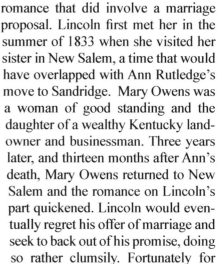

Mary Owens. This time it was a real romance that did involve a marriage proposal. Lincoln first met her in the summer of 1833 when she visited her sister in New Salem, a time that would have overlapped with Ann Rutledge's move to Sandridge. Mary Owens was a woman of good standing and the daughter of a wealthy Kentucky landowner and businessman. Three years later, and thirteen months after Ann's death, Mary Owens returned to New Salem and the romance on Lincoln's part quickened. Lincoln would eventually regret his offer of marriage and seek to back out of his promise, doing so rather clumsily. Fortunately for Lincoln, Mary Owens obliged him, accepting his withdrawal. Years later she wrote that "Mr. Lincoln lacked those little links that make up the chain of a woman's happiness."

One last point should be kept in mind when deciding if Abe and Ann were lovers or just friends. James Rutledge moved his family, including Ann, seven miles north of New Salem to a place called Sandridge in May 1833, meaning the two were physically present in New Salem for a period of only twenty-two months. And of those twenty-two months, John McNamar was present for the first twelve before leaving for New York. The period between McNamar's departure and Ann's departure saw Lincoln away on militia duty during the Black Hawk War. This places Ann and Lincoln together in New Salem for a period of only ten months. Any relationship between the two would have been carried out long distance. Roundtrip to Sandridge was fourteen miles and not something one would be expected to travel on a daily basis. Certainly Lincoln traveled to Sandridge to visit the Rutledge family. Enough evidence exists to support such travel. Whether it was to further romance or not is simply not known. The most important witness on this question is James Short who said he was unaware of any romantic relationship between the two and only after learning of Lincoln's grief after Ann's death concluded that there must have been something between the two to cause such despair on Lincoln's part.

One last point concerns Lincoln's presence at Ann's bedside just prior to her death. Two sisters, Nancy and Sarah Rutledge, responded to Herndon's inquiries about this point. That Lincoln was left alone in the room with Ann as she lay dying suggests that a personal relationship existed between the two. "I can never forget," Nancy Rutledge said years later, "how sad and broken-hearted Lincoln looked when he came out of the room." The fact that the Rutledges sent for Lincoln toward the end of Ann's life has some significance to those who believe the story.

To be fair to Herndon, he was not the first to bring the alleged romance to light. On February 15, 1862, four and a half years before Herndon's lecture, John Hill, the son of Samuel Hill and editor of the Menard (County) Axis newspaper located in Petersburg, Illinois, wrote an article titled "A Romance of Reality" in which he described an affair between Ann Rutledge and Lincoln. This early account would normally add credibility to the story except for the fact that John Hill was too young to be aware of any affairs in New Salem during the time of Lincoln and Ann's tenure in the village. He was born two years after Ann's death. Whatever Hill wrote about the couple was hearsay gathered years later, making Hill's recollections no better or no worse than Herndon's correspondents.

Mary Owens
Abraham Lincoln Presidential Library
and Museum

The controversy over the alleged love affair and engagement of Ann and Lincoln continues dividing historians, but not the general public. While the academy of historians debate the finer points of hearsay evidence the general public does not need convincing. For Lincoln to have loved and lost is the stuff legends are made of. Two young people thrown together in a small community sitting on the frontier adds plausibility to the legend. Adding to the legend are the several portrayals by Hollywood of the love affair, not to mention the beautiful young girls that have portrayed Ann Rutledge. The power of wanting to believe always wins over the logic of reason.

Twelve years after Ann's death, a married Lincoln visited his old home in Indiana where he saw an old friend who "unaccountably became furiously mad." That a person once quite normal should suddenly go mad both fascinated and haunted Lincoln. It inspired him to write a poem about the man titled "My Childhood-Home I see Again," but his words seem to go back to that August day in 1835 when death is thought to have pierced his heart for the third time.

O memory! Thou mid-way world
Twixt Earth and Paradise,
Where things decayed
and loved ones lost
In dreamy shadows rise.

Two lovers or two friends? In the end you will believe what you want to believe.

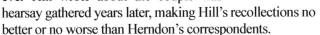

Lincoln writes to Mary Owens, carefully crafting his words about their tentative marriage. Lincoln clearly wants out of any commitment that may exist between the two. In the excerpt below, he begins with the rather strange salutation, "Friend Mary."

Springfield, August 16, 1837

Friend Mary,

I want at this particular time, more than anything else, to do right with you; and if I knew it would be doing right, as I rather suspect it would, to let you alone, I would do it. And for the purpose of making the matter as plain as possible, I now say that you can now drop the subject, dismiss your thoughts (if you ever had any) from me forever, and leave this letter unanswered, without calling forth one accusing murmur from me.

Further:

What I do wish is that our further acquaintance shall depend upon yourself. If such further acquain-

tance would contribute nothing to your happiness, I am sure it would not to mine. If you feel yourself in any degree bound to me, I am now willing to release you, provided you wish it; while, on the other hand, I am willing and even anxious to bind you faster, if I can be convinced that it will, in any considerable degree, add to your happiness.

If it suits you best to not answer this, farewell. A long life and a merry one attend you.

Your friend.
Lincoln

Years later in a letter to William Herndon, Mary Owens wrote, "I thought Mr. Lincoln was deficient in those little links which make up the chain of a woman's happiness."

Old Concord Cemetery

Located approximately three miles northwest of Petersburg nearly equidistant between that town and the Sandridge farm where James Rutledge moved his family in 1833, is a small pioneer cemetery known as Old Concord Cemetery. It is in many ways a mystical place, an island surrounded by farm fields and sheltered in part by a grove of honey locust and sycamore trees, immortalized by the burial of a young girl said to be the first and only love of Abraham Lincoln. Distant voices tell of a grieving Lincoln lying prostrate over the girl's grave wetting the soil with his tears. "My heart," he allegedly said, "lies buried here."

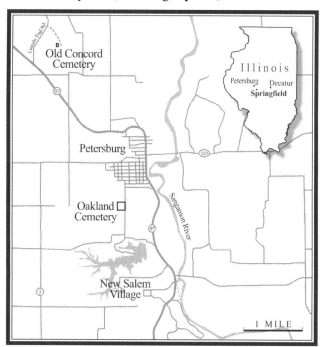

Old Concord remains one of those romantic memories that haunt the Lincoln story.

William Herndon described the cemetery in his famous Springfield lecture: "The cemetery contains about one acre of ground, and is laid out in a square. The dead lie in rows, not in squares, as is usual. In this lovely ground lie the Berrys, the Rutledges, the Clarys, the Armstrongs, and the Joneses, old and respected citizens, pioneers of an earlier day."

Purchased in 1826 by Samuel Berry, the cemetery has always resided on private land left undisturbed by the various farmers as they have gone about their work. On August 25, 1835, Ann Rutledge died at her home in Sandridge after lingering for several days with "brain fever," known today as "typhoid." She was buried in Old Concord among her New Salem neighbors. Seven years later her brother David, a former private in Captain Abraham Lincoln's company of Black Hawk militiamen, would die and be buried beside her.

Were Lincoln to return to the place of his alleged grief in search of the lovely Ann he would be told that she is gone, taken from her grave and carried off to the nearby town of Petersburg, where she now rests in Oakland Cemetery beneath a large granite marker. The robber of her grave was a man by the name of Samuel Montgomery, an undertaker and furniture dealer from Petersburg who owned an interest in the local cemetery. The slow sale of cemetery lots in Oakland prompted Montgomery to come up with a promotion that he believed would encourage sales. He hit on the idea of moving Ann Rutledge from Old Concord to Petersburg in the hope it would attract peoples' attention and spur sales.

Old Concord Cemetery as it appeared in 1993.

Montgomery needed the approval of Ann's next of kin or closest relative to remove her remains. McGrady Rutledge, then living in Petersburg, fit the bill. He was Ann's favorite cousin and the son of Ann's Uncle William Rutledge. Montgomery requested permission from McGrady Rutledge to exhume Ann. McGrady queried several Rutledge relatives all of whom were opposed to disturbing the grave. But Montgomery persisted, pressuring McGrady to give him permission to move Ann. Montgomery pointed out to McGrady that in Oakland Ann would be exposed to many more tourists than at Old Concord, and her grave at Oakland would be given perpetual care, something it would not get at Old Concord. Under Montgomery's pressure McGrady eventually gave in and Montgomery set about exhuming Ann and moving her to Petersburg.

Montgomery, along with McGrady, two of Montgomery's gravediggers, George Hollis and Peter Grosboll, and Hollis's young son James, set out for Old Concord. Since Ann's grave was no longer marked, Montgomery had to rely on McGrady, who was present at Ann's funeral, to point out the gravesite. McGrady told

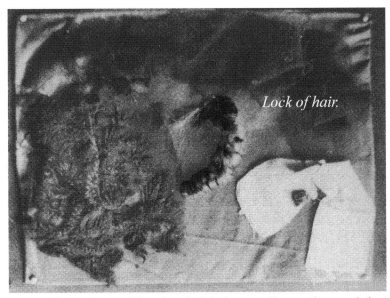

Lock of hair.

Preserved relics removed from Ann Rutledge's grave. From a photograph from the Menard-Salem-Lincoln Souvenir Album, *published by the Illinois Women's Columbia Club of Menard County, 1893.*

Montgomery that Ann was buried beside her brother David whose grave was marked by an engraved stone. But, McGrady did not know on which side of David Ann was buried. He did know that a small child was buried on one side with Ann on the other side. Montgomery's men be-

Anne Rutledge's grave at Oakland Cemetery, Petersburg, Illinois, shortly after her reinternment in 1890. Menard-Salem-Lincoln Souvenir Album, *published by the Illinois Women's Columbia Club of Menard County, 1893.*

gan digging and soon unearthed a small coffin containing the remains of a child. The men then started to dig on the other side of Ann's brother and soon came across the remains of a wooden coffin badly decayed. Montgomery's diggers removed two bones from the grave along with certain non-human items. The bones were a thigh bone (femur) and an upper arm bone (humerus). The non-human items consisted of a ribbon,

Samuel Montgomery's store wagon used to deliver furniture. Gary Erickson

pieces of black lace believed to come from Ann's dress, a small cloth-covered button, a roll of hair, a few pieces of wood from the coffin, and a bucket of dirt.

In an affidavit made in 1921 thirty-one years after the exhumation, Montgomery described the exhumation, stating that the "remains were removed as those of Ann Rutledge and buried in Oakland Cemetery where the marker now stands." In 1958, James Hollis, nine years old at the time of the exhumation, was interviewed by a "Lincoln student" from Petersburg named George Seipp. Hollis, now in his late seventies, told Seipp that "the incident is as vivid in his memory as if it happened yesterday." Hollis affirmed that only two bones were removed from the grave (a thigh bone and upper arm bone) along with hair that was "rolled up." Hollis went on to state that, "the bones, parts of the coffin, and the hair were put in a box and brought to Petersburg by Montgomery in his furniture wagon and there kept over night and the next day were taken to Oakland Cemetery and there buried."

This story of the reinternment of Ann Rutledge is troubling, to say the least. Two bones do not make a body. The human adult body consists of 206 separate bones. Why Montgomery removed only two bones from the grave is an open question. Were all 204 remaining bones dissolved such that Montgomery found only two, or was he so satisfied with the two bones that he stopped looking? From comments made by those present at the time it seems the latter is more probable. The picture is further complicated by the fact that certain of the articles removed from the grave never made their way to Oakland Cemetery.

In his detailed article in the *Lincoln Herald*, Gary Erickson writes that "the author has located a lady in Menard County who claims she has a lock of Ann's hair and buttons from Ann's dress, acquired from members of her family to whom they were given at the time of Ann's exhumation."

According to John Evangelist Walsh, author of *The Shadows Rise*, the lady is Margaret Richardson, a descendant of Jasper Rutledge, brother of McGrady Rutledge. The articles in Mrs. Richardson's possession are a small button (acorn shaped covered by cloth), a bow four inches long of silk-like ribbon, a strip of black lace two feet long, and a lock of hair two inches long. Interestingly, a photograph of identical items are shown in a photograph that appeared in a special souvenir album of Menard County published in 1893, only three years after the exhumation.

ON THIS VERY SPOT STOOD THE LOG CABIN IN WHICH ANN RUTLEDGE DIED AUGUST 25, 1835. ON THE HILLSIDE TO THE WEST STOOD A LARGE OAK TREE UNDER WHICH ABE LINCOLN BITTERLY WEPT AFTER LEAVING THE SICK ROOM OF ANN RUTLEDGE WHERE THEIR LAST COMMUNION WAS HELD

If the relics in the possession of Mrs. Richardson in 1993 are the items held out of the reburial of Ann Rutledge in 1890, it would appear that only two bones (of 206) along with a few pieces of wood and a bucket of soil were the only "remains" of Ann Rutledge reinterred in Oakland cemetery. It is doubtful that this constituted a "reburial" of Ann Rutledge.

Whether the alleged love affair and ultimate betrothal of Ann Rutledge and Abraham Lincoln is an historical illusion created by the imaginative mind of William Herndon or whether it is fact still escapes us after a century and a half. But one thing does seem certain in this great romantic story, and that is that the reinterment of Ann Rutledge to Oakland Cemetery is questionable. It seems more likely that Ann Rutledge rests among her friends and neighbors in her original burial place among the grove of trees at Old Concord Cemetery. If it is true that Abraham Lincoln walks at midnight, it is at Old Concord, and not Oakland, where he walks with Ann.

I am Ann Rutledge who sleep beneath these weeds

Out of me, unworthy and unknown
the vibrations of deathless music!
"With malice toward none, with charity for all."
Out of me forgiveness of millions toward millions,
And the beneficent face of a nation
Shining with justice and truth.

I am Ann Rutledge who sleep beneath these weeds,
Beloved of Abraham Lincoln,
Wedded to him, not through union,
but through separation.
Bloom forever, O Republic,
from the dust of my bosom!

Ann Rutledge grave in Oakland Cemetery in Petersburg. The large granite stone bears the poem by Edgar Lee Masters.

Above: Long view of Old Concord Cemetery
Right: Tombstone of David Rutledge, Ann Rutledge's brother. Died 1842.
Below: Early photograph of Old Concord Cemetery showing early wooden marker identifying the site of Ann Rutledge's grave. David Rutledge tombstone to the right of wooden marker.

Above left obverse: Modern stone marker replacing wooden marker over Ann Rutledge grave.

Above right reverse: The quotation on the stone is hearsay and cannot be directly attributed to Abraham Lincoln. Popularized by William Herndon through his interviews.

Right: Wooden marker identifying the original grave.

Below: Long view of Ann Rutledge grave.

Lincoln the Lover

The love story first introduced by William Herndon and made famous by Carl Sandburg did not rise to a high enough standard for most historians to be believable. The story was based on reminiscences recorded thirty years after the actual events took place and were the product of a man whose subjectivity occasionally got in the way of truth. The evidence was entirely circumstantial without a single document to back it up. That is, until the summer of 1928 when the Lincoln community, including its historians, was stunned by an amazing discovery: a cache of previously unknown letters between Lincoln and Ann Rutledge that left no doubt whatsoever that the two were not only deeply in love, but engaged to be married. Here was the documentary proof that even the most skeptical historian could not ignore.

Edward A. Weeks, the book division editor of the *Atlantic Monthly*, received a letter from a young woman inquiring about the eligibility requirements for an article in the magazine's non-fiction contest. The prize was $5,000 and open to all comers. The woman, Wilma Frances Minor, it turned out, had a collection of letters and diary entries that descended within her mother's family, which included love letters between Lincoln and

Ann Rutledge. She had written an article based on the documents and would like to submit it to the contest. Her revelation would be a bombshell within the literary world and Lincoln historical community. Somewhat stunned by Wilma Minor's letter, Weeks took it to Ellery Sedgwick, the *Atlantic's* senior editor.

Sedgwick was cautious, at first, and sought authentication of the documents. He turned first to William E. Barton, a tenacious researcher who had uncovered considerable material on his own. After looking over all the material, Barton gave his approval. The documents were real Barton said. Sedgwick next turned to Ida M. Tarbell, a well-known investigative journalist who had written an extensive biography of Lincoln. Tarbell concurred with Barton: "You have an amazing set of true Lincoln documents." To add icing to his cake, Sedgwick next turned to Lincoln biographer, Carl Sandburg. On examining the material, Sandburg was thrilled. Sandburg wrote to Sedgwick, "These new Lincoln letters seem entirely authentic – and preciously and wonderfully co-ordinate and chime with all else known of Lincoln." Barton, Tarbell, and now Sandburg had given their stamp of approval to the collection.

One fly in Sedgwick's ointment was Worthington Chauncey Ford, former head of the Manuscript Division at the Library of Congress. Like the other three Lincoln scholars, Ford was well versed in Lincoln and New Salem, having edited Albert Beveridge's two-volume biography of Lincoln. After examining photostatic copies of the material, Ford declared the letters forgeries. "They bear no resemblance to Lincoln's handwriting," Ford told Sedgwick. Shaken at first by Ford's response, Sedgwick ascribed Ford's negativity to jealousy.

Relying on three scholars' endorsements, Sedgwick went ahead with publication of the first of three planned articles under the title, "Lincoln the Lover."

The letters began "My beloved Abe," and "My beloved Ann," and often ended, "ever thine" and "with great affection, Abe." The three installments covered the early years in New Salem, the courtship, and the final tragedy. The story of Lincoln and Ann Rutledge's love affair was confirmed at long last thanks to the documentation of the love letters brought to light by Wilma Frances Minor.

But Ann's death was not the only tragedy the letters brought to light. Although the tragic love story surely warmed the hearts of Americans, it proved to be a fraud. A young and able Lincoln scholar named Paul Angle put his emerging reputation at risk by declaring the entire collection a fabrication and its owners as frauds. *Atlantic Monthly* and its readers had been the victims of a bad hoax.

Angle, secretary of the Abraham Lincoln Centennial Association, systematically shredded the documents by showing that several of the people who appeared in parts of the diaries and letters did not exist; they were creations of Wilma Frances Minor. A copybook allegedly used by Ann and described by her in a letter was not published until thirteen years after her death. References to Lincoln's surveys showed complete ignorance of survey designations. Trips to Kansas when Kansas did not yet exist as a state or as a territory belied the authenticity of the writer. Angle's careful fact-checking left no doubt in anyone's mind that the collection was a fabrication.

When confronted with the evidence, Wilma had a ready explanation. It seems her mother was a psychic who could speak with the dead; in particular, to Wilma's dead uncle. Wilma's mother would slip into a trance and communicate with the dead uncle who, it turned out, was able to communicate with Ann Rutledge and Lincoln, as well as other folks from New Salem. Wilma pointed out to Sedgwick that she, Wilma, was simply the conduit for Ann and Abe who related their love affair to the uncle who, in turn, related it to Wilma's mother. The sessions went on for weeks with Wilma's mother passing the information she gathered from the folks in New Salem along to Wilma who wrote it all down.

So you see, it was not a fraud, after all. Wilma was merely recording the words and thoughts of Abe and Ann as told to Wilma's

mother. All true, no lies. Wilma's mother was merely a "guide" to the wonderful story of "Lincoln the lover" and Ann Rutledge. What a wonderful opportunity for historians. They need only find the right medium to probe the past.

"Betrothal Stone."
This stone allegedly found by William Green near the Lincoln store in New Salem. The inscription reads: "A Lincoln Ann Rutledge were betrothed here July 4, 1833" *The stone, like the letters of Wilma Francis Minor, is a fabrication.* From Carl Sandburg, *The Prairie Years.*

"My Dearly Beloved Ann."
One of the forged documents from the Minor collection.

Frances Wilma Minor
from Don E. Fehrenbacher, The Minor Affair, R. Gerald McMurtry Lecture, *Fort Wayne, IN, 1979.*

The Continuing Education of Abraham Lincoln

By Lincoln's own admission, the aggregate of all his schooling did not amount to one year. Already able to read and write and cipher, Lincoln advanced his education considerably during the six years he lived in New Salem. Here he met Mentor Graham, himself a teacher of considerable skill who possessed a substantial library, substantial for frontier society. It was Mentor Graham who started Lincoln on the path to accumulating the skills he would display so eloquently in later years.

Not to be underestimated is the fact that five of Lincoln's New Salem neighbours had attended Illinois College and two had graduated from Dartmouth College. Graham also put Lincoln in touch with the Rodgers family who lived within walking distance from New Salem. The senior Rodgers owned an extensive library and his two sons were enrolled in medical school. All of these people were interested in intellectual pursuits, which fed Lincoln's own passion for knowledge.

It was Mentor Graham who told Lincoln that John Vance, who lived to the north of New Salem, had a copy of *Kirkham's Grammar*, which became the basis for Lincoln's writing skills. Lincoln would modestly write in 1860, "He regrets his want of education, and does what he can to supply the want."

Mentor Graham
National Archives

In 1834, after his little store "winked out," he secured a job as deputy to the county surveyor. Having no skills as a surveyor, he procured a compass and chain, studied *Flint and Gibson*, a little, and went at it.

Elected to the Illinois State Legislature in 1834, Lincoln came into close contact for the first time with John M. Stuart, an urbane lawyer and prominent Whig from Springfield, Illinois. The two men roomed together during the legislative session and Stuart encouraged Lincoln to study law. Sharing his law books and knowledge with the young Lincoln, Stuart would eventually hire him as a partner three years later, after Lincoln passed the bar examination and was admitted to practice in Illinois.

Lincoln was extremely resourceful and utilised every resource that was available to him. No experience, no matter how trivial, was left forgotten. He sought to learn from every experience and to add every opportunity to his growing store of knowledge. Beginning with Aesop and the Bible, he had an enormous capacity to remember what he had read and to use it at some point to illustrate or persuade. His intellect has intrigued every generation including his own and is a testament to his incredible capacity to learn and to apply the total accumulation of his learning to the matter at hand.

Mentor Graham's School. Used as a church on Sundays.

The Ploughman Poet and the Bard

While Lincoln owed much of his early education to Mentor Graham, it was Jack Kelso who introduced him to Shakespeare and Robert Burns. Both became his favorite and he read both with great enthusiasm, committing verse and dialogue to memory. Kelso could quote long passages from Shakespeare and the poems of Burns much to Lincoln's delight. It wasn't long before Lincoln was able to match Kelso and eventually surpass him.

In 1860, William Dean Howells published a campaign biography of Lincoln in which he wrote that Lincoln carried a copy of Burns's poems with him wherever he went while riding the Eighth Circuit as a lawyer. Howells sent Lincoln a copy asking him to edit it for accuracy. While Lincoln made several corrections, he let the Burns comment stand as written. Lincoln's attraction to Burns is obvious. Both began life in mudsill circumstances. Both were farmers early in life, and both were religious skeptics. While Burns was somewhere between an atheist and an agnostic, Lincoln was considered an "infidel" by those who knew, which is best described as a "Deist" rather than a Christian. More importantly, both men were steeped in democracy

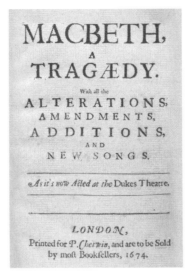

and an abiding love of the common man. Lincoln drew his political philosophy from the Declaration of Independence. A Scottish minister said of Burns that his poems set the Declaration of Independence to music.

Lincoln's other great love was Shakespeare, and while he admitted to not having read all of Shakespeare's plays he acknowledged having read several many times over, being able to quote them chapter and verse. Macbeth was Lincoln's favorite although Hamlet was a close second. In a letter to the great Shakespearian actor James Hackett, Lincoln wrote, "Some of Shakespeare's plays I have never read; while others I have gone over perhaps as frequently as any unprofessional reader… I think nothing equals Macbeth. I think it is wonderful." Concerning Hamlet, he wrote, "Unlike you gentlemen of the profession, I think the soliloquy in Hamlet commencing 'O, my offence is rank' surpasses that commencing 'To be or not to be.'"

The National Park Service recognized Lincoln's love of Burns by placing a bust of the Scottish poet in the parlor of the Lincoln home in Springfield, Illinois.

Lincoln's favorites: Jack Kelso, Robert Burns, and William Shakespeare.

A. Lincoln, Postmaster

Lincoln responds to George Spears's request for a receipt, adding "you wound my feelings."

Mr. Spears

 At your request, I send you a receipt for the postage on your paper — I am some what surprised at your request — I will however comply with it — The law requires News paper postage to be paid in advance and now that I have waited a full year you choose to wound my feelings by insinuating that unless you get a receipt I will probably make you pay it again —

   Respectfully
   A. Lincoln

Received of George Spears in full for postage on the Sangamo Journal up to the first of July 1834

   A. Lincoln P.M.

Letter from Matthew Marsh to his brother George M. Marsh bearing Lincoln's "Free" frank.

Free. A. Lincoln
New Salem
Sep. 22

Geo. M. Marsh
Portsmouth
N. H.

The Hill-McNamar (McNeil) store where most Lincoln historians believe Lincoln kept his post office.

A. Lincoln, Surveyor

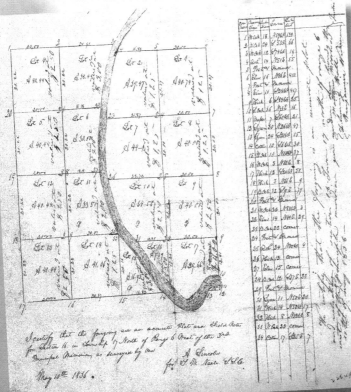

Failing in the store business, Lincoln watched as his possessions were sold at auction. His horse and surveying equipment were purchased by "Uncle Jimmy" Short who *"Uncle Jimmy" Short* promptly returned them to Lincoln. Lincoln's saddlebags and surveying instruments are on display in the New Salem visitor's center.

Above: *Survey conducted by Lincoln of Section 16 in Township 17 North of Range 6 West of the 3rd Principal Meridan, May 10th 1836.*
Right: *Lincoln the surveyor sculpture by John McClarey at Lincoln's New Salem State Historic Site in Petersburg. Commissioned by the Illinois Professional Land Surveyors Association.*
Lower Left: *Lincoln's surveying instruments on display at New Salem Visitors Center.*
Below: *Surveying text by Robert Gibson used by Lincoln to learn the theory and practice of surveying.*

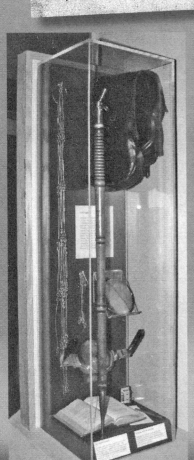

THE

THEORY AND PRACTICE

OF

SURVEYING;

CONTAINING

ALL THE INSTRUCTIONS REQUISITE FOR THE SKILFUL
PRACTICE OF THIS ART.

WITH A NEW SET OF ACCURATE

MATHEMATICAL TABLES.

BY ROBERT GIBSON.

ILLUSTRATED BY COPPER-PLATES.

NEWLY ARRANGED, IMPROVED, AND ENLARGED, WITH USEFUL
SELECTIONS,

BY JAMES RYAN,

NEW-YORK:

1832.

Lincoln Runs For Office

Politics was always Lincoln's ambition. He liked people, and people liked him, which is the first requirement to elective office. Lincoln's easy personality and good humor, as well as his intellect, made him an ideal candidate on the Illinois frontier. Unfortunately, few people outside of New Salem knew Lincoln well enough to support him in his effort to serve. Working against Lincoln's election was the fact that shortly after he decided to run for a seat in the Illinois legislature Black Hawk invaded Illinois, resulting in the governor calling for volunteers, taking Lincoln out of the race for several critical weeks.

Returning from the war in late July 1832, Lincoln set about campaigning. With only two weeks to go before election day, he had a difficult time canvassing his district. When the votes were finally tallied, only four seats were available out of the thirteen candidates running. Lincoln placed eighth, drawing 657 votes, well behind the fourth place finisher. Even so, he took great satisfaction in polling 277 votes out of 300 cast in his home district.

Having failed to win election to the state legislature, and in seeing his mercantile venture with William Berry "wink out," Lincoln was able to find work as postmaster and deputy surveyor during the summer of 1833. The meager earnings from both jobs were not enough to cover his substantial debt that forced his bankruptcy. The debt followed him for several years, but in the end, Lincoln paid off each of his debtors.

In the spring of 1834, Lincoln decided to make a second run for the state legislature. Although running as a Whig in a heavily Democratic district, Lincoln won election, polling the largest number of votes cast for any of the candidates. At the age of twenty-five, he was finally on his way to fulfilling his ambition of being first among many.

The state capital was the town of Vandalia, located in the southern half of the state some seventy-five miles southeast of Springfield and New Salem. Vandalia was the

The Vandalia State House, Illinois's fourth capitol. In 1836, Vandalia's leaders quickly built a new state capitol, hoping to persuade state legislators to keep the capital in Vandalia. Despite a new, spacious building, Lincoln, along with his Long Nine colleagues, moved the capital to Springfield.

western-most terminus of the National Road, a collection of existing turnpikes that ran from Baltimore to Vandalia. The road eventually made its way across the country, ending in San Francisco. Its principal advocate was Henry Clay who, along with Lincoln, championed "internal improvements" as essential to the economic growth of the country.

When Lincoln made his first visit to Vandalia the town had a population of six hundred people and some one hundred-odd buildings, mostly log cabins. Compared to places like New Salem, and even Chicago, at the time, Vandalia was a metropolis. Despite its frontier nature, the village had several amenities not found in other villages and towns around the state. It had several businesses including a capitol building, hotel, large tavern, furniture store, bookstore, and even a jewelry store. It was the site of several intellectual meetings, and most important to a young, naive Lincoln, it was the gathering place of the leading politicians and intellectuals from around the state. Finally, Lincoln could meet and talk with men of all backgrounds and interests stimulating his driving curiosity and allowing him to display his own intellectual prowess.

It was during Lincoln's campaign for reelection that he made an unusual, if not politically dangerous, declaration. Lincoln said, "I go for all sharing the privileges of the government, who assist in bearing its burthens. Consequently I go for admitting all whites to the right of suffrage, who pay taxes and or bear arms, by no means excluding females." These egalitarian views would eventually extend to black suffrage when on April 11, 1865, during a speech from the White House after Lee's surrender, Lincoln said, "It is also unsatisfactory to some that the elective franchise is not given to the colored man. I would myself prefer that it were now conferred on the very intelligent, and on those who serve our cause as soldiers." The words would ultimately lead to his assassination.

Lincoln soon joined with eight other Whig legislators who represented Sangamon County in the Illinois General Assembly during the 1836-37 legislative session. Lincoln and his eight Whig colleagues quickly became known as "The Long Nine." All nine representatives were over six feet in height, unusual for the 1830s. Together, the Long Nine were able to successfully maneuver a bill through the legislature, establishing Springfield as the state capital.

During the ten-week legislative session Lincoln joined with his Black Hawk War comrade, John Todd Stuart, who, two years later, when Lincoln moved to Springfield, took Lincoln on as his law partner in the firm of Stuart and Lincoln. Lincoln had earned his license to practice law in September 1836, seven months before moving to Springfield. It was at this time that Lincoln helped engineer moving the state capitol from Vandalia to Springfield.

Vandalia had ceased to be a "modern" capital, being remotely located and serviced by poor roads, poor climate, poor lodging, and poor food. Stuart complained that the only food in town were "prairie chickens and venison." It took Lincoln and his Long Nine colleagues most of their political capital to convince the legislature to move the capital to the growing city of Springfield but, in the end, they were successful. The vote to relocate passed in February 1837 and, two weeks later, Lincoln packed his entire inventory into two saddle bags and rode out of the dying village of New Salem into the promising town of Springfield. His pioneer past behind him, Lincoln was ready to begin his climb toward the presidency.

Original dais in the Vandalia State House.

Here I have lived...

Springfield
1837-1861

*Here I have lived a quarter of a century,
and have passed from a young to an old man.*

Abraham Lincoln

When Abraham Lincoln rode into Springfield in April 1837, he found a town that had grown remarkably since it's founding just sixteen years earlier. Springfield was eight years older than the village of New Salem, but unlike New Salem, had grown and prospered since its founding. While New Salem was slowly dying, Springfield burst with growth and commerce. The town had been surveyed as early as 1821, but the first land sales didn't take place until 1823. Elijah Iles was Springfield's founder and first merchant.

Iles, along with three other settlers, purchased the first quarter sections from the United States government all centered on the town square, which had been laid out by Iles's survey of two years earlier. Having staked out their claim, the four entrepreneurs had town lots laid out, which were then offered for sale at prices ranging from a low of fifteen dollars to a high of fifty dollars. Situated strategically on the southeast corner of the new town square was the mercantile establishment of Iles. Iles was more interested in land sales than clerking, but nevertheless built a general store on the corner near the surveyors stake laying out the center of the new town. In a memoir written many years later, Iles told of his Springfield beginnings.

> *After I got to Springfield in 1821, and explored the country to some extent, I determined to make this section my permanent home; my intention was farming, but as the land was not yet in market, I erected a cabin, sixteen feet square, with sheds, and went to St. Louis and bought a general assortment of goods, and opened the first store in Springfield, in June, 1821.*

They commenced to call me old

Lincoln's life in Springfield can be broken down into three distinct parts. The first took him from his arrival in 1837 through his term as Congressman in 1849. During this time, Lincoln was active politically, establishing himself as a force within the Illinois Whig party. The second part of his life in Springfield was from 1849 until 1854 when Lincoln seemed to fall away from national politics and to devote most of his time and energy to his law practice, where he proved successful both in court and at the bank. The world, it seems, had passed him by, taking his passion for politics with it. Others saw a once promising star fade, but not Mary Lincoln. She never lost sight, or hope, for her brilliant husband.

In 1854, the passage of Stephen Douglas's Kansas-Nebraska bill overturning the Missouri Compromise defining the limits of slavery so angered Lincoln the lawyer that he returned to politics with a new enthusiasm that delighted his friends and scared his opponents. Thus began the third phase of his Springfield life. Douglas's bill would reverse the agreement to designate the territories, Kansas and Nebraska, free from slavery to one in which the residents could vote slavery up or down as they chose. Douglas had called his new policy "popular sovereignty." Lincoln called it treachery. The Missouri Compromise allowed Missouri to enter the Union as a slave state while prohibiting slavery in the rest of the Louisiana Purchase. The period from 1854 to 1860 saw Lincoln emerge as the leader of Illinois's Whig Party and, ultimately, the country's Republican Party.

Slavery once again raised its ugly head, stirring a dormant Lincoln. He hated slavery. "I hate it," he said, "because it deprives our republican example of its just influence in the world . . . [and] causes the real friends of freedom to doubt our sincerity." A southerner by birth, Lincoln knew that the "peculiar institution," if allowed to spread into the territories, would eventually consume the entire country. It must be stopped, and now. This new compromise opened the floodgates, trampling on past agreements and setting the cause of abolition back decades. While slavery had been a political force for the past seventy-five years, it would now consume all of politics. Not a bill passed through the Congress, no matter how innocuous, without being scrutinized as to its possible effect on the institution of slavery.

When Lincoln arrived in Springfield in April of 1837, he moved in with his closest friend, Joshua Speed. The two men shared a bed located in a small room over top of Speed's store, which became a part-time hangout for several young men in Springfield who would eventually go on to greater things. Lincoln had received his license to practice law before leaving New Salem and on arriving in Springfield became a partner with John Todd Stuart.

From a young...

Iles and his colleagues were, in fact, squatters when they first settled down around the square. With no one opposing their bids, the originators of Springfield purchased their quarter sections at the minimum rate of a dollar and twenty-five cents an acre.

In 1823 the town was nothing more than a frontier hamlet with a few log dwellings scattered around the muddy square. Now, fourteen years later, Lincoln found a bustling, cosmopolitan community, and it was to his liking. Established as the county seat in 1825, Lincoln, now a state legislator from New Salem, had personally engineered the transfer of the state capital from Vandalia to Springfield in March 1837. One month later, he left New Salem, and took up residence in the town he helped make the Illinois capital. Having become both county seat and state capital, Springfield would prove just the place for the budding Lincoln's new career as lawyer and politician.

Lincoln lived a total of twenty-four years in Springfield. Here he met his wife Mary, was married, saw four children born and one die, established a career as a successful attorney, and emerged the political leader of two parties in succession, the dying Whig party and the new rising Republican party. Springfield played a major, if not dominant, role in Lincoln's rise to national fame.

when I was scarcely thirty.

Stuart was a well-established lawyer and important Whig, both of which served Lincoln well in his new town. The two men first met when they served in the Black Hawk War five years earlier.

Two years after Lincoln's arrival, Mary Todd arrived in Springfield from Lexington, Kentucky, and moved in with her sister and brother-in-law, Frances and Ninian Edwards. Lincoln and Edwards were allies in the Illinois state legislature, and it was not long before the mixing of social and political events brought Lincoln and Mary Todd together. Although the couple shared little in common among the superficial traits so obvious to their friends, they shared a passion for politics and intellect. The two became fast friends and soon became a couple, eventually becoming engaged.

A wedding date was set for January 1, 1841, but was cancelled at the last minute. Exactly what happened to cause the cancellation of their marriage is not known for certain, but most historians fault Lincoln for the breach in the relationship. Perhaps doubts set in; perhaps the thought of marriage terrified Lincoln, no one knows for sure, only that the couple separated and Lincoln became "the most miserable person on the face of the earth." Some historians believe Lincoln actually loved another woman while others believe he panicked at the thought of marriage. Eventually brought back together through the efforts of their common friend, Simeon Francis, the two lovers decided to try again and set a new date for November 4, 1842. This time the wedding went forward and Abraham and Mary started on a new career melding family, law, and politics into one.

For the next eleven years, the Lincolns flourished. Mary gave birth to four sons, tragically losing the second son, Edward Baker Lincoln, or Eddie, when he was only six years old, in 1850. Lincoln served two more terms in the state legislature before his election to the United States Congress in 1846. His two years in Congress were rather uneventful save for his opposition to the Mexican War. On December 22, 1847, Lincoln introduced a resolution demanding that President James Polk show Congress the very spot on American soil where Mexicans had attacked American soldiers. It became known as the "Spot Resolution." While Lincoln's opposition to the war hurt him initially, it soon faded away and did him no damage in his future quest to run for the senate and eventually the presidency.

Returning from Washington in 1849, he drifted away from politics, devoting his time to his law practice and becoming one of the city's more successful lawyers. In 1854, Stephen A. Douglas, chairman of the Senate Committee on Territories, engineered the Kansas-Nebraska Act, which effectively repealed the Missouri Compromise

...to an old man.

of 1820 banning slavery above the 36-30' parallel. Northerners saw this Act as favouring southern slave interests and breaking a compromise that all parties had accepted in an effort to suppress extremists on both sides of the issue. Lincoln, in his own words, was "thunderstruck" by Douglas's actions. Having slowly drifted way from politics on his return from Congress, Lincoln now re-entered the political arena with a fury.

In 1856 Douglas became a candidate for the Democratic nomination for President, while Lincoln became a candidate for vice president on the new Republican Party ticket. Both men failed in gaining their parties endorsements, but only momentarily. Douglas remained among the more prominent Democrats and a front-runner for the 1860 nomination. Lincoln's stature was also growing rapidly. The first meaningful contest came in 1858 when the Illinois Republican Party, on June 16, 1858, chose Lincoln as their "first and only candidate" to run against the "Little Giant" for the Illinois senate seat. The nomination was misleading in that senators were chosen by their respective state legislatures. While Douglas and Lincoln were the endorsed candidates of their respective parties, the real contest would be to elect state legislators who supported one or the other candidate.

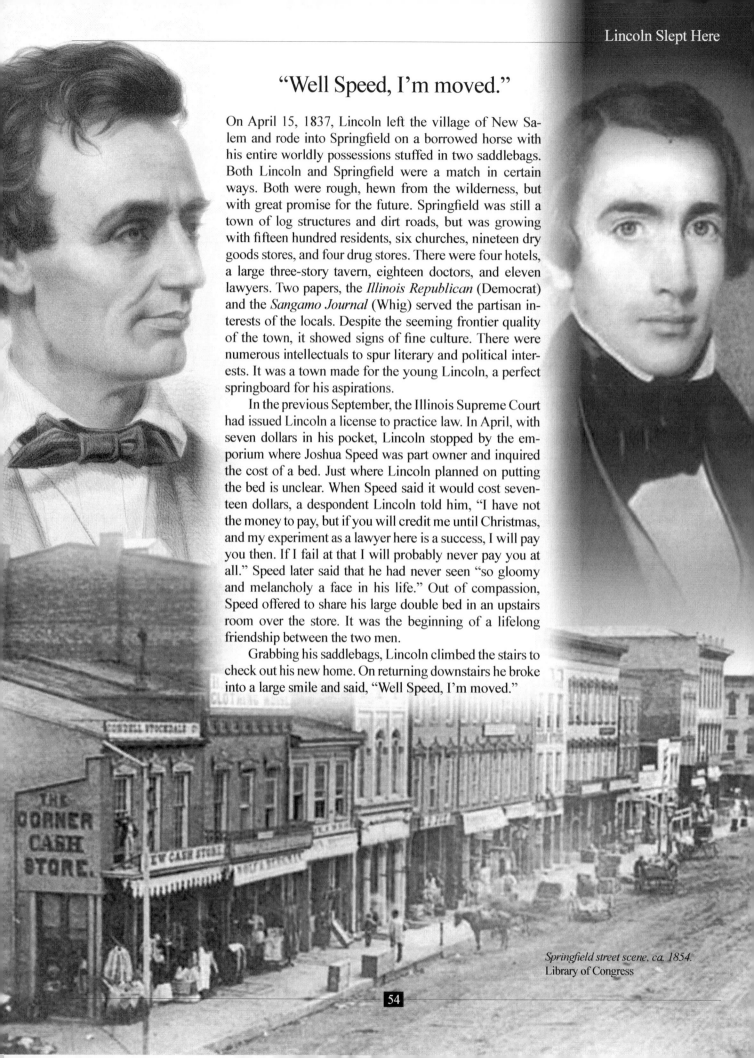

"Well Speed, I'm moved."

On April 15, 1837, Lincoln left the village of New Salem and rode into Springfield on a borrowed horse with his entire worldly possessions stuffed in two saddlebags. Both Lincoln and Springfield were a match in certain ways. Both were rough, hewn from the wilderness, but with great promise for the future. Springfield was still a town of log structures and dirt roads, but was growing with fifteen hundred residents, six churches, nineteen dry goods stores, and four drug stores. There were four hotels, a large three-story tavern, eighteen doctors, and eleven lawyers. Two papers, the *Illinois Republican* (Democrat) and the *Sangamo Journal* (Whig) served the partisan interests of the locals. Despite the seeming frontier quality of the town, it showed signs of fine culture. There were numerous intellectuals to spur literary and political interests. It was a town made for the young Lincoln, a perfect springboard for his aspirations.

In the previous September, the Illinois Supreme Court had issued Lincoln a license to practice law. In April, with seven dollars in his pocket, Lincoln stopped by the emporium where Joshua Speed was part owner and inquired the cost of a bed. Just where Lincoln planned on putting the bed is unclear. When Speed said it would cost seventeen dollars, a despondent Lincoln told him, "I have not the money to pay, but if you will credit me until Christmas, and my experiment as a lawyer here is a success, I will pay you then. If I fail at that I will probably never pay you at all." Speed later said that he had never seen "so gloomy and melancholy a face in his life." Out of compassion, Speed offered to share his large double bed in an upstairs room over the store. It was the beginning of a lifelong friendship between the two men.

Grabbing his saddlebags, Lincoln climbed the stairs to check out his new home. On returning downstairs he broke into a large smile and said, "Well Speed, I'm moved."

Springfield street scene, ca. 1854.
Library of Congress

54

On the Rise

If destruction be our lot, we must ourselves be its author and finisher.
As a nation of freemen, we must live through all time, or die by suicide.

Abraham Lincoln, *Lyceum Address, January 17, 1838*

Nine months after arriving in Springfield and joining the law firm of John T. Stuart, Lincoln addressed the Young Men's Lyceum of Springfield. It was his first major address before a large crowd on a sub-

☞ THE YOUNG MEN'S LYCEUM will meet at the usual time and place. In compliance with the request of the Lyceum, A. LINCOLN, Esq. will deliver an Address to the members of that body on Saturday evening the 27th inst. The public are invited to attend.
By order of the Lyceum. J. H MATHENY, Sec'y.

Sangamo Journal advertisement of Lincoln's speech to the Young Men's Lyceum.

followers pledged no compromise when it came to slavery versus abolitionism, even if it meant disregarding the law.

ject Lincoln felt passionate about, and reverence for the law. Although not an abolitionist in practice, Lincoln was an abolitionist in heart. Slavery had dominated politics for most of the century, pitting abolitionists on the left with pro-slavery people on the right. This battle basically pitted Whigs against Democrats. Caught in the middle were the great masses of Americans, neither abolitionists nor pro-slavery people. State and Federal legislatures were often bound up in a tangled morass of arguing over slavery. In most instances, bills introduced before any legislature, state or federal, were scrutinized for their possible negative effects on slavery. Arguments became heated, while public gatherings frequently erupted in violence.

In April 1836, Francis McIntosh, a free black in St. Louis, became involved in a street fight trying to protect two citizens in which a policeman was stabbed to death. McIntosh was arrested and confined in the local jail; a mob broke into the jail and dragged McIntosh to the edge of town where they chained him to a tree and burned him to death.

Several months later, Elijah Lovejoy, a Presbyterian minister and newspaper editor who published abolitionist articles, was repeatedly attacked by angry mobs. Three of his printing presses were destroyed. Despite the continuing threat to his business and his life, Lovejoy did not back down. On November 7, 1837, Lovejoy was murdered in Alton, Illinois, while attempting to prevent a mob from destroying his newly purchased printing press. These two episodes of mob violence in total disregard for the law spurred Lincoln to make his first major speech. While many believed that both McIntosh and Lovejoy had brought about their own deaths by their actions, Lincoln profoundly disagreed. Mob violence and disregard for the law were an anathema to Lincoln. These acts, Lincoln said in his speech, were "the effects of mob law... There is no grievance that is a fit object of redress by mob law." Lovejoy, Lincoln said, had every right to free speech without fear of physical reprisal. John C. Calhoun, known as the "cast-iron man" for his uncompromising defense of slavery and opposition to abolitionism, said that "reasoning down" abolition was "absurd." Calhoun and his

Lincoln told his audience, "Let every lover of American liberty, every well-wisher to his posterity, swear by the blood of the Revolution, never to violate in the least particular, the laws of the country; and never to tolerate their violation by others." Lincoln went on to give one of his most stirring words in defense of the nation's laws:

Let reverence for the laws be breathed by every American mother, to the lisping babe that prattles on her lap – let it be taught in the schools, in seminaries, and in colleges; let it be written in Primers, spelling books, And in Almanacs; let it be preached from the pulpit, proclaimed in legislative halls, and enforced in courts of justice. And, in short, let it become the political religion of the nation; and let the old and the young, the grave and the gay, of all sexes and tongues, and colors and conditions, sacrifice unceasingly upon its altars.

Lincoln's Lyceum speech catapulted him to the forefront of his party and established him as a careful and thoughtful person dissecting complex issues, reducing them to their very core such that two farmers mending a fence could understand the basic issues. It also pitted Lincoln against the Democrat's emerging leader, Stephen A. Douglas. The two rivals would oppose one another up every rung of the political ladder until one day they reached the very top.

The Baptist Church where Lincoln delivered his "Lyceum Speech".
Library of Congress

You must remember that some things that are legally right are not morally right.
Abraham Lincoln

Lincoln the Lawyer

*Law is nothing else but the best reason of
wise men applied for ages to the transactions
and business of mankind.*
Abraham Lincoln

In an unusual reversal of the accepted practice of the day, Lincoln became a politician before he became a lawyer. He entered politics officially in 1832, five years before he was admitted to practice before the bar. Having just returned from service in the Black Hawk War, Lincoln ran for the state legislature, coming in seventh out of twelve candidates. Although he did not win a seat, he was greatly encouraged by winning 277 out of 300 votes cast in New Salem. Failing in his first effort to become a state legislator, Lincoln tried again in 1834, this time winning. In 1836 Lincoln was re-elected, having served two years to most everyone's satisfaction.

Established as a politician, Lincoln decided to take up the law. During the Black Hawk War he became acquainted with Springfield attorney John Todd Stuart, a cousin of Mary Todd. Now, both men were serving in the Illinois state legislature together. Impressed with Lincoln's analytical mind and intellect, Stuart encouraged him to pursue the law. Lincoln had already undertaken some study as far back as Indiana where he had read the *Revised Statutes of Indiana* and *Blackstone's Commentaries* while clerking in New Salem. Lincoln would journey to Springfield and visit Stuart's office where he would borrow law books from Stuart's library.

On September 6, 1836, Lincoln finally applied for a license to practice law and on March 1, 1837, received his license. On April 15, 1837, Lincoln left New Salem and rode into Springfield to start a new life. He was now employed in the prestigious law firm of John Todd Stuart. For the next four years Lincoln prospered under Stuart, gaining expertise as a trial lawyer. In January 1840 he made his first appearance before the Illinois Supreme Court. The case was dismissed on Lincoln's motion. Although Stuart was an excellent lawyer whose office handled many cases, Lincoln disliked the routine legal work that Stuart gave him. He wanted more from the law. Following Stuart's absence in Washington as a congressman, Lincoln approached Stuart about his future in the firm. After four years with Stuart, the two men parted amicably and Lincoln joined the firm of Stephen T. Logan. Logan was an excellent lawyer and not interested in political office. He devoted most of his time to his practice and Lincoln benefited greatly from Logan's attention to the practice. In 1844, Lincoln and Logan separated. Logan wanted to take on his son as his partner and the firm could not support three partners. Lincoln took on the twenty-six-year old William Herndon as his new partner, forming the firm of Lincoln and Herndon. It would last until Lincoln's death in 1865.

When Lincoln left for Washington as President-elect he told Herndon to keep the old "Lincoln and Herndon" sign hanging outside the door to their office. "If I live," Lincoln told his partner, "I'm coming back some time, and then we'll go right on practicing law as if nothing had ever happened."

John Todd Stuart
Illinois State Historical Library

Stephen T. Logan
Illinois State Historical Library

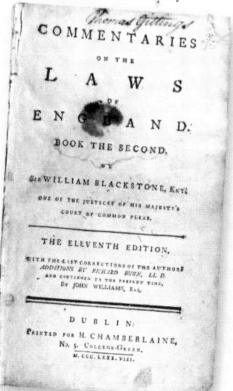

Blackstone's Commentaries

Lincoln's Eighth Judicial Circuit

At the time Lincoln was admitted to the bar in 1837, Illinois consisted of seven judicial circuits each presided over by a judge appointed by the state legislature. Lawyers moved from town to town within each circuit trying cases as they moved. Between 1837 and 1839 the state legislature created twenty-one new counties, necessitating the creation of two new circuits, the Eighth and the Ninth. The Eighth, Lincoln's circuit, was made up of eight counties with a total population of 41,000 people. The circuit court began in the spring in Springfield and moved progressively through the eight counties before returning to Springfield where a second session of the court was held. The fall term of the court began in Springfield in September and followed the same circuit as in the spring, ending up back in Springfield in November. The entire route traveled by Lincoln covered just over two hundred miles and lasted between seven and eight weeks. By 1843, the state legislature expanded the circuit to fourteen counties extending the circuit traveled to 450 miles. The area covered 15,000 square miles encompassing a full one-fifth of the state. The new circuit required Lincoln to be away from home for twelve weeks out of the year.

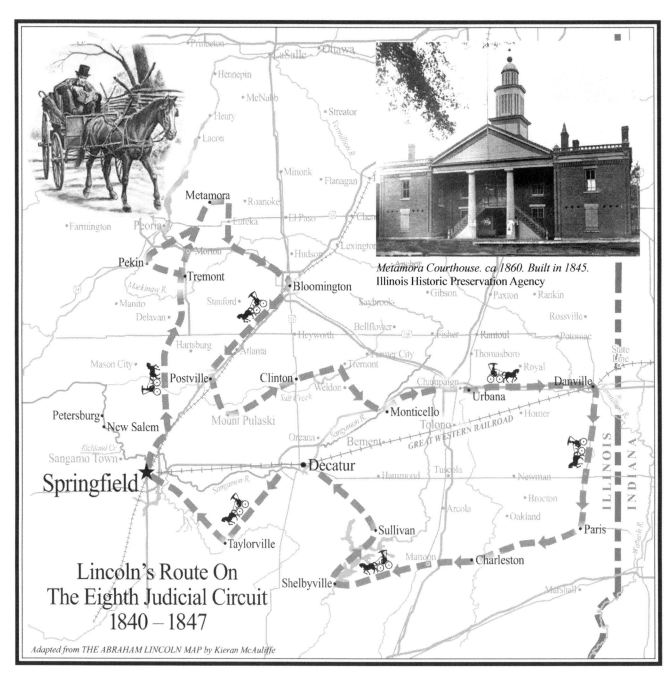

Metamora Courthouse. ca 1860. Built in 1845.
Illinois Historic Preservation Agency

Lincoln's Route On
The Eighth Judicial Circuit
1840 – 1847

Adapted from THE ABRAHAM LINCOLN MAP by Kieran McAuliffe

Courthouses varied greatly over the Eighth Circuit, ranging from simple one-room log cabins to substantial brick buildings. In Danville, court was held in what was originally the log cabin home of the county sheriff. In Paris, the Edgar County Courthouse was a large two-story brick building built in 1833. Over the years most of the original log buildings were replaced with large, two-story brick buildings.

Edgar County Courthouse in Paris, Illinois, 1862. A company of Union soldiers assemble at the Courthouse in April 1862, shortly before leaving for Pittsburg Landing, Tennessee, with medical supplies, following the battle of Shiloh, April 6 and 7. It is the earliest photograph of the courthouse where Lincoln practiced law.

Postville Courthouse (reconstruction). Lincoln practiced law in this courthouse from 1840 to 1848. Postville was the Logan County seat located twenty-five miles north of Springfield.

McLean County Courthouse, Bloomington, Illinois. Built in 1835, the McLean County Courthouse rivaled the Edgar County Courthouse in size and architecture. It replaced a more modest log structure.

Eighth Circuit Historical Marker. In the 1920s historical markers were placed along the route Lincoln and his fellow lawyers traveled riding the Eighth Judicial Circuit. The marker reads, "Abraham Lincoln traveled this way as he rode the circuit of the Eighth Judicial District 1847-1859."

Danville Hotel

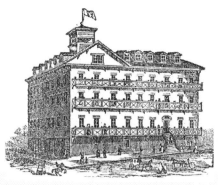

Bloomington Hotel

Metamora Courthouse

Petersburg Courthouse

Clinton Courthouse

Logan County Courthouse

Lincoln Circuit Rider
bu Fred M. Torrey
in the Lincoln Tomb
in Springfield.

William Henry Herndon. Lincoln's Last Law Partner.

*If I live I'm coming back some time, and then we'll go right on practicing law
as if nothing had ever happened.*

Abraham Lincoln

In 1844, Lincoln chose a young, newly licensed lawyer named William Herndon as his law partner. Years later, when asked why Lincoln chose him, Herndon replied, "I don't know and no one else does." Herndon served as the office manager of the Lincoln-Herndon practice, carrying out a significant part of the research that went into the two men's cases. While Lincoln traveled the Eighth Circuit arguing cases, Herndon remained in Springfield taking care of the business.

Like it or not, and many historians do not like it, Herndon is the principal source, and in many instances the only source, of our view of Lincoln. Within a few weeks of Lincoln's death, Herndon embarked on a crusade to gather as much information about his partner and friend from everyone and anyone who touched Lincoln's life. Herndon sought out dozens of people by letter and interview, gathering every scrap of data concerning Lincoln. Planning on writing a "true history" of Lincoln including the "unvarnished truth," Herndon soon became the "informant" through which recollections and reminiscences were channeled. Without Herndon, our knowledge of Lincoln, even in those earliest days of his life, would be woefully lacking.

Not always reliable, Herndon appears to be most controversial in his portrayals of Lincoln and Ann Rutledge, and in his views of Mary Lincoln. Historians remain almost evenly divided on the alleged love affair between Lincoln and Ann Rutledge. As to Mary Lincoln, the two disliked one another in a most personal way. "Mrs. Lincoln," Herndon said, "is a very curious – excentric [sic] – wicked woman. Poor Lincoln! He is domestically a desolate man." To Herndon, Mary Lincoln was, "the female wildcat of the age."

Mary Lincoln was no shrinking violet when it came to Herndon, who she banned from the Lincoln home. In response to Herndon's lectures disparaging the marriage between Mary and her husband, Mary wrote, "This is the return for all my husband's kindness to this miserable man! Out of pity he took him into his office, when he was almost a hopeless inebriate." She thought he was nothing more than "a dirty dog."

An alcoholic most of his life, Herndon went sober in 1881 and saw his dream of writing a biography realized with the publication of "*Herndon's Lincoln. The True Story of a Great Life,*" written in conjunction with Jesse W. Weik. The book did little to bolster Herndon's reputation. Herndon died in 1891, two years after the book's publication.

The collected papers of Herndon (mainly preserved in the Library of Congress) were published by Douglas L. Wilson and Rodney O. Davis in "Herndon's Informants" published by the University of Illinois Press in 1998.

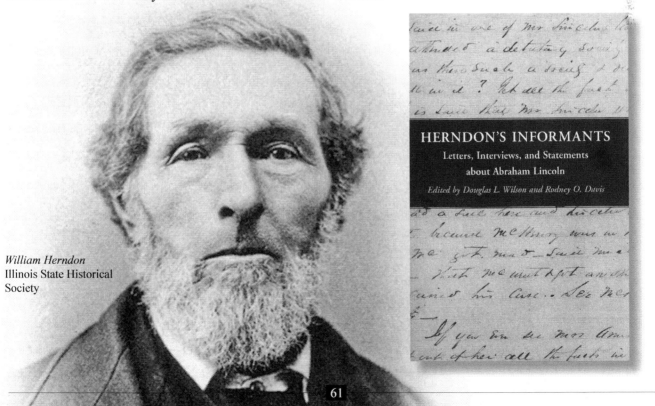

William Herndon
Illinois State Historical
Society

HERNDON'S INFORMANTS
Letters, Interviews, and Statements
about Abraham Lincoln
Edited by Douglas L. Wilson and Rodney O. Davis

Congressman Lincoln
1847-1849

Lincoln's political ambitions took a setback in 1846 when the then Whig member of Congress, John J. Hardin, decided to run for the seat in Illinois's seventh congressional district. Lincoln had an understanding that the congressional seat would rotate by agreement between Hardin, Edward Baker, and Lincoln, but Hardin claimed he made no such agreement. He would seek another term ignoring Lincoln's claim. The seat was currently occupied by Baker who acknowledged the agreement and agreed not to seek reelection. In May of 1846, pushing Hardin aside, the delegates at the Whig convention unanimously chose Lincoln as their congressional candidate. The Democrats selected the famous Methodist preacher, Peter Cartwright, to oppose Lincoln.

Lincoln ran a masterful campaign against the older preacher. Just when it appeared Lincoln would easily roll to victory Preacher Cartwright accused Lincoln publically of being an "infidel," a non-believer who mocked Christian-

Peter Cartwright

ity. This was a serious charge with political implications. Cartwright charge that Lincoln was a "scoffer" of religion was gaining ground among many Whigs, forcing Lincoln to reply to Cartwright's charges. Timing his response to a week before the election, Lincoln distributed a handbill stating his position: "That I am not a member of any Christian Church, is true; but I have never denied the truth of the Scriptures; and I have never spoken with intentional disrespect of religion in general, or of any denomination of Christians in particular."

One Sunday during the campaign Lincoln attended a revival meeting in Springfield where Cartwright was holding forth. Seeing Lincoln in the audience Cartwright renewed his attack on Lincoln's alleged infidelity. Pointing directly at Lincoln, Cartwright asked, "If you are not going to repent and go to Heaven, Mr. Lincoln, where are you going?" Lincoln won the crowd over with his answer, "I am going to Congress, Brother Cartwright."

Lincoln's disavowal of Cartwright's charges worked. Lincoln defeated Cartwright by just over 1,500 votes, the largest margin for that district ever. In December 1847, Lincoln was off to serve in the Thirtieth Congress on his way to an even greater political career, or so he thought.

"Spotty" Lincoln

Mexico has passed the boundary of the United States, has invaded our territory and shed American blood on American soil.

President James K. Polk

And whereas this House desires to obtain a full knowledge of all the facts which go to establish whether the particular spot of soil on which the blood of our citizens was so shed was, or was not, our own soil.

Abraham Lincoln

On April 25, 1846, a patrol of American cavalry was attacked by a contingent of Mexican troops in a region between the Nueces River and the Rio Grande River, a region traditionally claimed by Mexico. The incident followed a series of negotiations in which the Polk administration had attempted to purchase the land and

President James K. Polk

was rebuffed. The United States Congress, with President James K. Polk's forceful backing, then declared war on Mexico, claiming that Mexican troops had invaded United States territory and spilled American blood on American soil. In his speech to the Congress calling for war against Mexico, Polk submitted a resolution stating, "Whereas, by the act of Mexico, a state of war exists between that government and the United States."

A few weeks later Lincoln rose on the floor of the House and delivered a speech demanding that Polk tell the Congress "the particular spot of soil on which the blood of our citizens was so shed," and whether the soil "was our own soil." The resolution submitted by Lincoln became known as the "Spot Resolutions," and Lincoln became known as "Spotty" Lincoln. The resolution was never brought to the floor for a vote and died, never to be mentioned again. Whether Lincoln's opposition to the war damaged his future political career is doubtful. He did not run again for political office until 1854 when he was elected to the Illinois State legislature. He was defeated that same year in an attempt to seek the Whig nomination for the United States Senate, losing to Lyman Trumbull.

PLUCKED :
THE MEXICAN EAGLE BEFORE THE WAR!   THE MEXICAN EAGLE AFTER THE WAR!

Washington, D.C., 1847-1849

The Capitol Building at the time of Lincoln's stay in Washington had a wooden dome clad in copper. Expansion of the building, including a grand new dome, began in 1854 and was still incomplete in 1861. Library of Congress

Mrs. Sprigg's boarding house (second from left) across from the Capitol where the Lincolns lived. Mary, Robert and Eddie soon left to stay with her sister in Lexington, Kentucky. Library of Congress

Mexican American War

*I have to say I am in favor of General Taylor as the Whig candidate
for the presidency because I am satisfied we can elect him.*

Congressman Abraham Lincoln

During Lincoln's first year in Congress he found himself in a political fight to elect the Mexican War hero, Zachary Taylor. Although Lincoln vigorously opposed the war, he decided to support the war's hero, Taylor, who considered himself an Independent but sided with the Whig Party on key issues. Lincoln told his fellow Whigs that he was "satisfied we can elect him."

Following Taylor's victory at Buena Vista, political groups began forming to nominate him as a Whig for the presidency. Even though thrice-defeated Henry Clay, Lincoln's "Beau Ideal," decided to make a fourth run for the Whig nomination, Lincoln threw his support to Taylor because Clay, Lincoln said, "stood no chance at all" of winning. Taylor won the nomination with little difficulty and went on to defeat the Democratic candidate, Lewis Cass.

Lincoln campaigned vigorously for Taylor, remaining in Washington during the summer months. He spoke to crowds in Washington and Rockville, Maryland, charming audiences with his wit and humor. Lincoln slowly gained recognition and popularity for his speaking ability as he toured the Northeast stumping for Taylor. Following his speech in Boston, the *Boston Atlas* praised Lincoln, writing that he delivered "one of the best speeches ever heard in Worcester."

While Lincoln's campaigning exposed him to many of the leaders of the Whig Party that would serve him years later, he failed to gain the recognition with the Taylor administration that he sought. Assuming he had earned a patronage position, Lincoln wound up with nothing for his hard work.

It was during his return trip to Illinois during the Congressional break that the steamboat Lincoln was on ran aground on a river sandbar. Intrigued by the boat captain's use of empty barrels to help lift the boat off of the bar, Lincoln returned home to prepare his patent titled "Improvement for Buoying Vessels."

Zachery Taylor
Whig candidate in 1848

Lewis Cass
Democratic candidate in 1848

Battle of Buena Vista, Library of Congress

Lincoln Secures a Patent

Lincoln's fascination with innovative technology manifested itself on several occasions. In 1858 and 1859 he prepared and delivered a formal lecture in Springfield, titled *Discoveries and Inventions*. One of the most visited places by Lincoln during his presidency was the Washington Navy Yard where he witnessed the testing of new weaponry.

An interest in invention came to fruition in 1849 when he submitted a patent application for lifting boats that had run aground. He received his patent in May 1849, the only president to secure a patent.

Lincoln's idea for his invention appears to stem from an incident that occurred while he traveled from Washington back home to Springfield at the close of his first session in Congress in 1848. The boat he was traveling on ran aground, and the captain of the vessel freed it by tying empty barrels onto the hull and floating the boat off the sandbar.

When Lincoln arrived home he sought the help of a local mechanic and built a model containing "buoyant chambers" attached to the ship's hull. By a system of pulleys and spars the chambers would be inflated and forced into the water, raising the boat and thereby freeing it. Although issued, the patent was never used.

No. 6469.—*Improved method of lifting Vessels over Shoals.*
What I claim as my invention and desire to secure by letters patent, is the combination of expansible buoyant chambers, placed at the sides of a vessel, with the main shaft or shafts C, by means of the sliding spars or shafts D, which pass down through the buoyant chambers, and are made fast to their bottoms and the series of ropes and pulleys, or their equivalents, in such a manner that by turning the main shaft or shafts in one direction, the buoyant chambers will be forced downwards into the water, and at the same time expanded and filled with air for buoying up the vessel by the displacement of water, and by turning the shaft in an opposite direction, the buoyant chambers will be contracted into a small space, and secured against injury.
A. LINCOLN.

Above right: *Lincoln's Patent Application.* NARA
Center right: *Publication of Lincoln's Patent No. 6469. Published in the annual report of the Commissioner of Patents, 1849.*
Center: *Patent Office Building, now the Smithsonian National Portrait Gallery and American Art Museum. Built in 1837, the building was used for Lincoln's inaugural ball following the 1864 election. Photo: John Plumbe, 1846. Library of Congress.*
Below: *Lincoln's patent model, currently in the Smithsonian Institution. The Lincoln Museum, Fort Wayne, IN.*

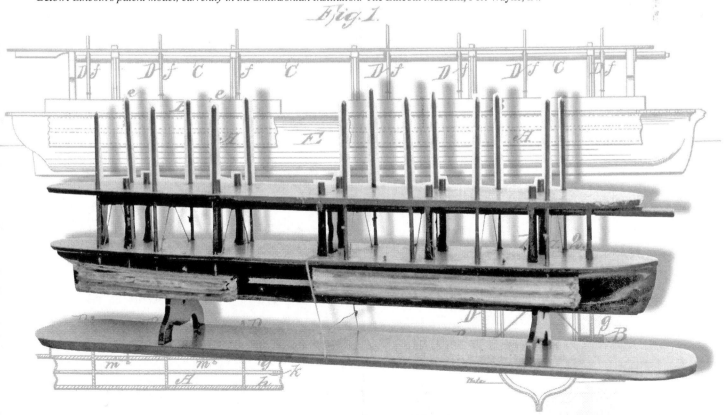

The Almanac Trial

I've danced that boy on my knee a hundred times in the long winter nights by his father's fire.
Abraham Lincoln on Duff Armstrong

The famous wrestling match between Abraham Lincoln and Jack Armstrong in the village of New Salem in 1831 had far reaching effects on both Lincoln and the Armstrong family. In September 1857, Duff Armstrong, Jack and Hannah's son, got into a brawl at a camp meeting after heavy drinking and caused the death of James Preston Metzker. Duff, along with a man named James Norris, were indicted for Metzker's murder and brought to trial in Beardstown, Illinois, on May 7, 1858. Lincoln, made aware of the trial, agreed to join Armstrong's counsel and defend the young Duff Armstrong out of deep respect for his mother and father, Jack Armstrong, who had died a few months before.

The principal witness for the prosecution, Charles Allen, claimed he saw both Norris and Armstrong savagely hit the drunk Metzker about the head, causing fractures that resulted in Metzker's death three days later. Cross-examined by Lincoln on the witness stand, Allen maintained he clearly saw the attack because of the moonlight that illuminated the scene. Lincoln pressed his examination vigorously, "Are you certain there was a moon that night?" Allen answered, "Yes, sir; I am certain." Lincoln pressed on, "You are sure you are not mistaken about the moon shining as brightly as you represent?" Again Allen answered, "No, sir; I am not mistaken." Lincoln then asked, "About what time did you say this [attack] happened?" Allen answered, "About 11 o'clock at night."

Lincoln then produced an 1857 almanac showing that the moon had set at 12:10 a.m. and was so low on the horizon as to be blocked by the trees in the area. Allen's credibility was suddenly shattered, throwing his entire testimony in doubt. After considerable deliberation, the jury returned a verdict of "not guilty."

With the passing years the case grew in fame and embellishment, becoming known as "The Almanac Trial." There is no doubt that self-defense was not the case, and Duff Armstrong and James Norris were guilty at least of manslaughter. In a separate trial, Norris was found guilty and sentenced to eight years. After the acquittal, Lincoln grabbed hold of Duff and told him to go home to his mother and "be a good boy."

Duff Armstrong
Illinois State Historical Library

Above left: *Ambrotype by Abraham Byers, May 7, 1858.* Courtesy Lloyd Ostendorf.

Above right: *Hannah Armstrong, wife of Jack Armstrong and mother of Duff Armstrong.* Illinois State Historical Library.

Lower left: *Interior of the Beardstown courtroom where trial was held.*

Lower right: *Cass County Courthouse, Beardstown, Illinois. Built 1844.*

Lincoln's Springfield

Springfield is my home, and there, more than elsewhere, are my life-long friends.

Abraham Lincoln

Founded in 1821, the city of Springfield's population was a scant six hundred individuals when Lincoln arrived in 1837. In 1839, with the support of the "Long Nine" delegates, he had convinced his fellow legislators to move the Illinois capital from Vandalia to Springfield. The village became a perfect fit for Lincoln.

A newly licensed lawyer and state legislator, Springfield and Lincoln grew together to become Illinois's greatest monuments. The four paintings depicted here are believed the work of French artist Mathuren Andrieu, created sometime between 1850 and 1854. They depict the "four sides of Springfield" as viewed from the cupola of the Old State Capitol. Sections of the roof appear in each painting. Their historic value is considerable, showing the city at a time when Lincoln was at the height of his legal career. The paintings hang today in the Old State Capitol.

View looking east, ca. 1854. The columned buildings are the courthouse (left) and the Marine Fire and Casualty Company (right) where Lincoln did his banking.

The four images shown here are courtesy of the Sangamon County Historical Society.

View looking south, ca. 1854. The prominent building in the lower section of the picture contained the law offices of Lincoln and Herndon.

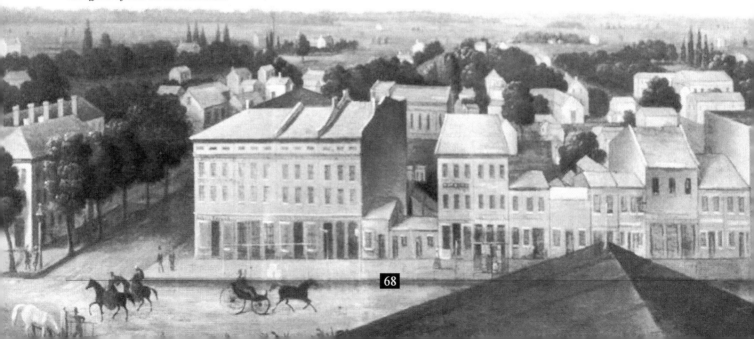

View looking west, ca. 1854. The two churches seen in the picture are Springfield's two Presbyterian churches. On the left is the Second Presbyterian Church; on the right is the First Presbyterian Church, the church the Lincolns attended.

View looking north, ca. 1854. The large building in the lower left section of the painting contained Lincoln's first law office as a partner of John T. Stuart.

The Lincoln Family

Abraham Lincoln and Mary Todd were married on November 4, 1842, in the home of Mary's sister and brother-in-law, Elizabeth and Ninian Edwards. The decision to marry appears to have been made hastily even though the two had shared a long courtship that had seen the couple separate for a period of time. Mary informed her sister on the morning of November 4 that she and Lincoln would marry that same evening. The Edwards were not in favor of the marriage, believing the two were not suited for one another and nothing good would come of the marriage. Mary was determined and her sister set about trying to put together a wedding party with only a few hours' notice. By evening everything was under control and the wedding took place to everyone's satisfaction. The newly married couple set up housing in the Globe Tavern where they lived until moving into the house on Eighth and Jackson.

The earliest known images of Lincoln and Mary. These are daguerrotypes believed to have been taken in 1846, four years after the couple married. At the time Lincoln was thirty-seven and Mary twenty-seven-years-old. Years later Mary remarked that "They are very precious to me, taken when we were young, and so desperately in love."

Robert Todd Lincoln, *the eldest son. Born 1843, died 1926. Robert was the only surviving son to marry and have children. The line of descent ended with Robert Lincoln's grandson Robert Todd Lincoln Beckwith who died in 1985.*

William Wallace "Willie" Lincoln. *Born 1850, died 1862. Young Willie fell ill in the White House in February, 1862, and died of typhoid fever.*

Thomas "Tad" Lincoln. *The youngest of the four Lincoln boys, he was nicknamed "Tad," which was short for "tadpole." Like three of his brothers before him, Tad died prematurely at the age of eighteen.*

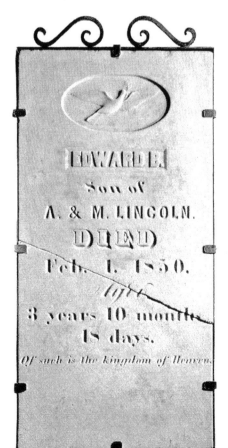

Fido, the Lincoln's pet dog. Left behind with a neighbor, Lincoln had the dog's photograph taken so the boys would have his image while in Washington. A year after Lincoln's assassination, Fido was killed by a drunken man who stabbed the dog after he had playfully put his dirty paws on the man.

Edward Baker Lincoln, *The Lincoln's second child died in 1850 from tuberculosis, two months shy of his fourth birthday.*

SPRINGFIELD
ILLINOIS · 1860

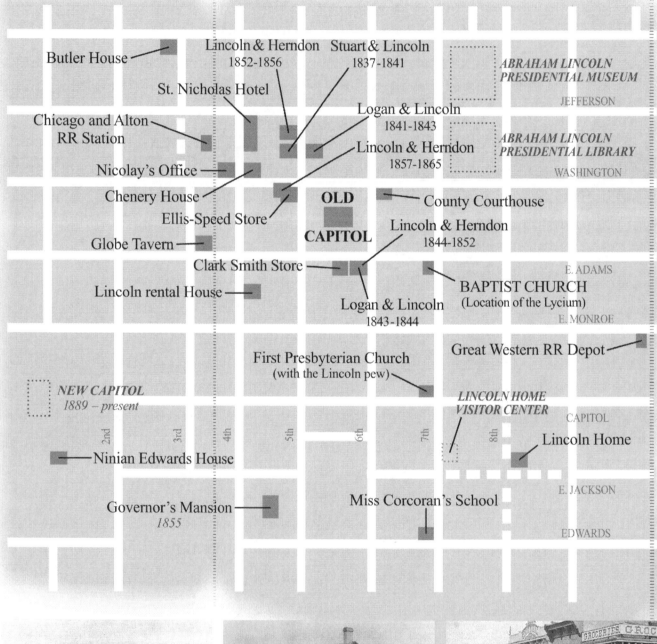

Butler House

Lincoln & Herndon
1852-1856

Stuart & Lincoln
1837-1841

*ABRAHAM LINCOLN
PRESIDENTIAL MUSEUM*

JEFFERSON

St. Nicholas Hotel

Logan & Lincoln
1841-1843

Chicago and Alton
RR Station

*ABRAHAM LINCOLN
PRESIDENTIAL LIBRARY*

WASHINGTON

Lincoln & Herndon
1857-1865

Nicolay's Office

Chenery House

OLD

County Courthouse

Ellis-Speed Store

CAPITOL

Lincoln & Herndon
1844-1852

Globe Tavern

E. ADAMS

Clark Smith Store

BAPTIST CHURCH
(Location of the Lycium)

Lincoln rental House

E. MONROE

Logan & Lincoln
1843-1844

Great Western RR Depot

First Presbyterian Church
(with the Lincoln pew)

NEW CAPITOL
1889 – present

*LINCOLN HOME
VISITOR CENTER*

CAPITOL

2nd

3rd

4th

5th

6th

7th

8th

Lincoln Home

Ninian Edwards House

E. JACKSON

Governor's Mansion
1855

Miss Corcoran's School

EDWARDS

Globe Tavern where Robert Lincoln was born on August 1, 1843.
Illinois State Historical Library.

Following their wedding at the home of Ninian Edwards, the new-lyweds took up residence in the Globe Tavern located two blocks west of the public square in Springfield. The Lincoln's would live at the Globe until the fall of 1843. In a letter to his close friend Joshua Speed, Lincoln wrote, "Our room and boarding only costs four dollars a week." The Lincoln's first child, Robert, was born at the Globe Tavern on August 1, 1843. Despite the modern concept of a tavern rooming house, the Globe was a major establishment and had been home to several prominent Springfield persons, including John Todd Stuart and Dr. William Wallace.

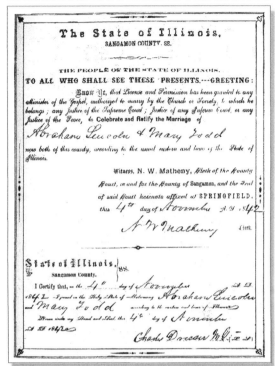

Marriage license of Abraham Lincoln and Mary Todd.

Lincoln's only home

When Abraham and Mary Lincoln purchased their house in 1844 from the Reverend Charles Dresser, the minister who had married them, it was a one-and-a-half story, five-room cottage. The cottage was built in 1839 and was located in what today would be considered an upper class neighborhood. The full second story was not added until 1856, and then, at the insistence of Mary Lincoln. The surrounding yard was devoid of any landscaping and at times both the yard and the house showed signs of neglect due to Lincoln's indifference to such things. The enlarge-

Sketch of Lincoln home before remodeling took place. Lincoln purchased the one-and-a-half story house in 1844 from Reverend Charles Dresser, the man who married the Lincolns.

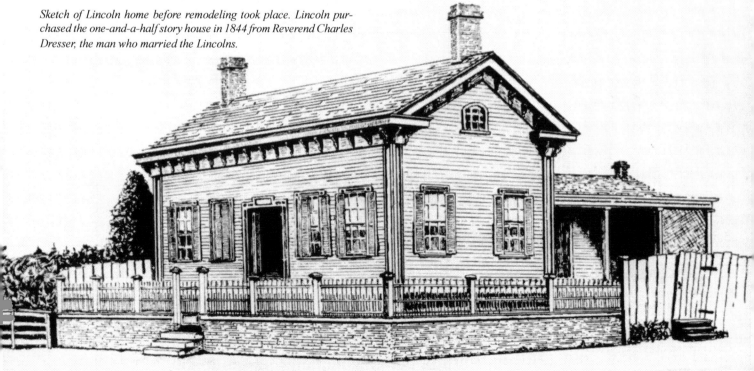

Osborn H. Oldroyd

A.LINCOLN

Name plate from Lincoln home.

ment of the house provided more room than the Lincolns needed for their family and they took on a boarder. Mary Lincoln had a maid named Mariah Vance who worked for the family at various times between 1850 and 1860 and lived-in for a period of time. The house was located at Eighth and Jackson streets, a short distance from Lincoln's law offices.

Built in 1839 by the Reverend Charles Dresser, the Lincolns lived in the house from May 1844 until leaving for Washington in February 1861. Lincoln leased the home to Lucian Tilton for $350 a year. Tilton, president of the Great Western Railroad, lived in the house until 1869 when George Harlow moved in. Robert Lincoln specified that he did not want any changes made to the house or the property of "a permanent character."

In 1877 Jacob Akard, a sewing machine salesman, moved into the house with his wife and two young children. Akard apparently turned the home into a boarding house, renting out several of the rooms.

The house fell into a state of disrepair due to neglect and hard use by the tenants. It sat vacant for a while before Robert Lincoln offered it to the Lincoln Monument Association. The Association declined Robert's offer, stating that they had their hands full administering the Lincoln Monument.

Robert had repairs done to the house and cleaned it up before finding another occupant. In 1879, Dr. Gustav Adolph Hermann Wendlandt, a physician and highly educated man, moved into the Lincoln home. Wendlandt and his wife lived in the home until 1883 when Osborn H. Oldroyd and his wife Lida moved in. The year before Oldroyd had rented the Charles Arnold house located on the southeast corner of 8th and Jackson, opposite the Lincoln home. Oldroyd displayed his ever-expanding collection of Lincoln memorabilia in the front and rear parlors and opened it to tourists, charging them a fee.

Oldroyd had agreed to pay Robert Lincoln $25 a month, but within a year he had fallen in arrears, which it seems Robert Lincoln forgave. Oldroyd began lobbying for the state to take over the home and appoint Oldroyd custodian. At first Robert Lincoln did not want to sell the property, but in 1887 changed his mind. The state offered to purchase the home, but Robert responded by stating that if the state agreed to preserve the house "as an object of public interest" he would donate the property. The property was acquired by the state on June 16, 1887, and Oldroyd was retained as custodian with a salary of $1,000 per year. In 1888 the state appropriated funds for "repair and maintenance."

In 1892, Democrats swept all of the state offices, including the governorship, which the Republicans had held since 1857. Oldroyd, a staunch Republican, was told to gather up his collection and vacate the premises. Oldroyd moved his large collection of Lincoln artifacts into a vacant home two blocks west of the Lincoln Home.

Oldroyd was out of work, with his collection sitting in storage, when the Memorial Association of the District of Columbia asked him to bring his collection to Washington and display it in the Petersen House where Lincoln died. The Petersen had stood empty and closed to the public. Oldroyd and his collection were the perfect match for the sacred house that stood across the street from Ford's Theatre.

Oldroyd moved into the house and opened his exhibit to the public on October 17, 1893. On October 7, 1896, the United States government purchased the Petersen House from the Memorial Association and Oldroyd became its permanent occupant and custodian.

Back in Springfield, Herman Hofferkamp became the new custodian of the Lincoln home. Hofferkamp, the beneficiary of the Democratic takeover of the state government suffered his predecessor's fate when the Republicans returned to power in the 1896 election and Hofferkamp was dismissed. On July 1, Albert S. Edwards, the son of Ninian Wirt Edwards, Mary Lincoln's brother-in-law, was appointed the new custodian of the home.

Following Edwards' death in 1915, a series of state appointed custodians administered the home until August 18, 1971, when President Richard Nixon came to Springfield. Sitting at the desk used by President-elect Abraham Lincoln to draft his inaugural address, he signed the bill authorizing the Secretery of the Interior of the United States to establish the Lincoln Home National Historic Site under the National Park Service.

The Lincoln home and surrounding four-block area has been under the administration of the National Park Service since 1972. In 1987, the Park Service began a complete renovation and structural rehabilitation of the house. Several tenants lived in the home after the Lincolns moved to Washington in 1861. From 1883 to 1892, Lincoln collector Osborn H. Oldroyd displayed his extensive collection of Lincoln artifacts in the house. In 1893 Oldroyd moved his collection to Washington where he displayed it in the Petersen House where Lincoln died. In 1887 Robert Lincoln donated the house to the state of Illinois.

Massachusetts Congressman George Ashmun, head of the committee that notified Lincoln of his nomination as the Republican Party candidate for the presidency, later commented on the house: "Everything tended to represent the home of a man who has battled hard with the fortunes of life, and whose hard experience has taught him to enjoy whatever of success belongs to him, rather in solid substance than in showy display." Another member of the committee referred to the house as "handsome, but not pretentious." Congressman W.A. Richardson of Illinois was less tactful in his comments: "The scene around his home betrayed a reckless indifference to appearances."

First Floor

Above: On May 19, 1860, Lincoln greeted a special ten-member committee that had come to Springfield to inform him that he had been nominated as the Republican Party's candidate for the presidency. The committee, led by chairman George Ashmun of Massachusetts, consisted of the heads of various state delegations. The committee arrived shortly after eight o'clock in the evening. Ashmun introduced each member to Lincoln, who formally accepted the nomination. Lincoln, a non-drinker, served the committee cold water. The front parlor is now furnished with period pieces based on contemporary sketches of the room. The over-size sofa (rear left) and Mary Lincoln's what-not cabinet (rear right) are two of the Lincoln's original possessions.

Below left: The original stove in the kitchen. Below right: The front hall and stairs leading to the second floor.

Second Floor

Above: Lincoln's bedroom. Mary Lincoln's bedroom is seen through the open door connecting the two bedrooms.
Below: Lincoln's bedroom. The chest of drawers and chair are original pieces. The rest of the furniture is authentic to the period when the Lincolns lived in the house.

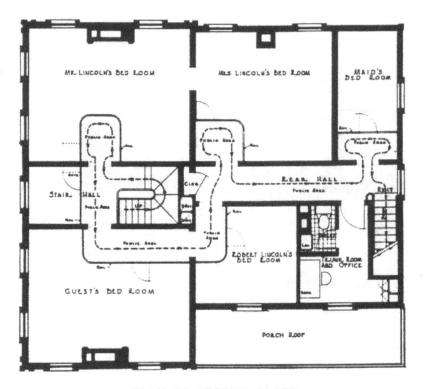

PLAN OF SECOND FLOOR

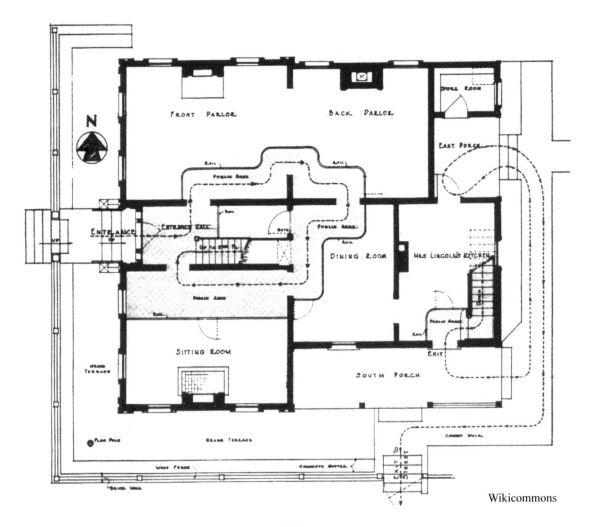

Lincoln's Neighborhood

Charles Arnold House. *Arnold, a member of the Whig Party and later Republican Party, was a close political ally of Lincoln. The home is located directly across Jackson Street to the south of the Lincoln home.*

Charles Corneau House. *Corneau was in partnership with Roland Diller, Lincoln's druggist. The house is located on Eighth Street catty corneer from the Lincoln house.*

Lyon House. *Henson Lyon was a retired farmer. By 1860, at the time of Lincoln's election to the presidency, Lyon, his son, Thomas, Huldah Burge and her three children, and three other persons resided in the structure. The house is located across Eighth Street from the Lincoln house.*

Mary Todd, Kentucky Scion

In her bearing she was proud, but handsome and vivacious.
William H. Herndon

To most people who had any reasonable acquaintance with Mary Todd and Abraham Lincoln, their eventual marriage would seem absurd at best. Lincoln, at six feet, four inches, towered over the foot shorter Mary Todd who stood just under five feet four inches tall. The lanky Lincoln had virtually no formal education to speak of and lacked training in even the rudimentary rules of social graces. He had no experience or opportunity to practice the social graces common to Mary Todd's world. His awkward appearance was in stark contrast to Mary's graceful and coquettish features. Lincoln's hardscrabble frontier upbringing had taught him much about life close to nature, but in the finer elements of societal living, he was woefully deficient.

Mary Owens had said of Lincoln, "I thought Mr. Lincoln was deficient in those little links which make up the chain of a woman's happiness." Mary Todd was as at least as astute as Mary Owens and considerably more demanding of those little links in her own chain of happiness. But the seeming differences between the two were more than outweighed by the attraction they felt for one another and the similarities that they shared, not the least of which was ambition. Both shared a driving ambition to succeed. Both shared a passion for politics and political leadership.

Mary Todd was born on December 13, 1818, in Lexington, Kentucky, to one of the richest and most priviledged families in the South at a time when the young Abraham Lincoln was still mourning the death of his mother in Indiana. Lexington was as far removed from the wild frontier of Indiana as it was from Paris, France. Mary's father, Robert Smith Todd, was among Lexington's most influential and successful men, whose family was among the elite of Kentucky. The Todd-Stuart-Edwards-Clay-Parker-Humphreys families read like a who's who of American aristocracy. Power and influence were their hallmarks. That Abraham Lincoln was able to crack through this wall of privilege attests to the value the elite placed on intelligence.

Robert Todd and his first wife, Eliza Parker Todd, had six children survive, among them Mary. Eliza died when Mary Todd was only six, and her father remarried soon after her death. Robert and his second wife bore eight children who became half brothers and half sisters to Mary. Mary adored her mother and was deeply wounded by her death. This became all the more important in her young life because her new stepmother showed little interest in her or her siblings. Such neglect only steeled the young girl's ambition to succeed. In Abraham Lincoln, Mary saw success, and she liked it.

While Lincoln went to school "by littles," Mary studied at one of the finest girls schools in the country, Madame Mentelle's School for Girls. At the time, education in Lexington was the equal of that found in Boston; so much so, that Lexington was often referred to as "the Athens of the West." Here Mary became among the more highly educated young women of her day. Schooled in the classics, she became fluent in French under the careful tutelage of Madame Mentelle.

In 1837, at the age of nineteen, Mary visited Springfield for the first time where her sister Elizabeth lived following her marriage to Ninian Wirt Edwards.

An unusual portrait carte de visite of Mary Lincoln. Date and photographer unknown.

Mary Lincoln in a black taffeta dress. The photograph was taken by Matthew Brady in 1861.

Although Mary visited her sister around the time Lincoln came to Springfield, it is not known whether they ever met during her first visit. The fact that Lincoln was a political colleague of Edwards, and served with him in the state legislature for two terms, makes it probable that he and Mary met at the Edwardses house sometime during Mary's first visit.

In 1839, Mary, now twenty-one-years old, moved to Springfield permanently and took up residence in the home of her sister and brother-in-law. Having met the young Mr. Lincoln, Mary was strangely attracted to him. The refined and socially prominent Edwards liked Lincoln as a political ally and friend, but felt that he was no match for the cultured and well-bred Mary. Mary's interest in Lincoln was discouraged at every turn, but with little success. The attraction between the two transcended the elitism of Kentucky's Brahmans. Only two years after his breakup with Mary Owens, Lincoln fell in love with Mary Todd, and she with him. The two young lovers

soon became engaged and set their marriage for January 1, 1841, only to have it broken at the last moment. Lincoln biographers have had a field day describing the humiliated Mary standing pitifully at the altar waiting for Lincoln to show. In truth, there is no evidence to suggest that preparation for a wedding ceremony ever took place or that anything other than a mutual agreement to end the engagement took place. Others claim Lincoln had fallen in love with Matilda Edwards, Ninian Edwards young and beautiful cousin, and told Mary he could not marry her. Like so many stories about Lincoln, this too falls under hearsay with questionable provenance. The point is, the couple reunited after a few months and married.

Whether the break up of Lincoln and Mary Todd was mutual is not clear, but it proved only momentary, however, as the two were reunited through the efforts of their close friends, Simeon Francis and his wife. This time, the young lovers kept their wedding plans secret and announced them only on the day they were sched-

TODD HOUSE

HOME OF MARY TODD LINCOLN FROM 1832 TO 1839. TO THIS HOUSE IN AFTER YEARS SHE BROUGHT ABRAHAM LINCOLN AND THEIR CHILDREN.

uled to be married. The Edwards, realizing that Mary could not be dissuaded, insisted that the young couple hold their ceremony in the Edwards home that same evening.

Mary Todd and Abraham Lincoln were married on November 4, 1842, nearly two years after their first scheduled wedding. Why they decided to marry is something of a mystery since their backgrounds were so dissimilar. But, as is often the case, love requires no reason.

The young couple boarded at the Globe Tavern in Springfield where they lived for the next two years. Here their eldest son, Robert Todd Lincoln, was born on August 1, 1843, nine months after their marriage. In 1844, the family moved into the only home they would ever own, located at Eighth and Jackson Streets near the heart of Springfield. A one-story house, Lincoln would add a second floor and expand the modest home into one of Springfield's finer houses. For the next seventeen years, the family thrived with the addition of three more sons. The first of Mary's several tragedies struck when the second of her four children, four-year-old Eddie, died in 1850.

The Lincolns life in Springfield was marked by Lincoln's growing success as both a lawyer and a politician. By the summer of 1860, Mary Lincoln was eager and well prepared to assume the role of first lady to her presidential husband. What she was not prepared for was the unrelenting attacks on her husband's abilities and integrity and on her own loyalties as the southern first lady of a divided nation. The White House years were increasingly difficult for Mary Lincoln as she became increasingly erratic in her behavior. The death of her third son in 1862 came close to pushing her over the edge. A sufferer of migraine headaches, the pressure of politics, the constant criticism by her and her husband's critics, and the death of young Willie Lincoln only heightened Mary's mood swings. An intellectually astute woman who loved to engage in conversational jousting, Mary experienced the criticism associated with Victorian attitudes and mores when it came to intellectual women. Although she made many enemies, she also made a few friends. She was a woman who was both hated and loved, sometimes for the same reasons.

On that fatal night in April 1865, she witnessed the murder of her husband who had been the stabilizing force in her life. Within a period of fifteen years she had lost two young children to disease and her husband to an

The Todd house became a commercial residence and storefront before being saved as a historic site.

assassin. These tragedies pushed her to the brink of her sanity, and without the protective shield of her powerful husband to care for her, her enemies took every advantage of her vulnerable position.

Mary eventually left the country, taking her young boy Tad with her to Germany in 1868. In 1871 she returned to the United States only to see her "darling Tad" die in July the same year from what appears to have been tuberculosis. After the death of her Eddie and Willie, and her husband, Tad had become her emotional center. Mary Lincoln had said earlier, "Only my darling Taddie prevents me from taking my life." Now she told her closest friends, "As grievous as other bereavements have been, not one great sorrow, ever approached the agony of this."

By 1875, Mary's only surviving son Robert became increasingly alarmed at her behavior. He attempted to force his deteriorating mother to gain psychiatric care, and failing that, took steps to secure control over her finances before she lost everything. After an unseemly court battle, he had her committed to a private sanatorium in Batavia, Illinois. Robert's action remains controversial among some to this day. Charges that Robert sought to take over his mother's finances for his own use are clearly unfounded. Mary Lincoln exhibited signs of psychoses, its cause not completely clear. There is reason to believe she had become dependent on paregoric, a medicine containing opium, commonly used in small doses to treat coughing spasms in children. Uncontrolled use frequently led to addiction and erratic behavior. Mary showed all the signs of opium abuse.

Mary appears to have benefited considerably from her hospitalisation and after four months was released to the care of her sister and brother-in-law, Elizabeth and

Mary Lincoln was concerned about her image. She tried to control the photographic images made of her through such letters as the following, addressed to Henry T. Anthony, successor to Matthew Brady in New York City.

Dear Sir

At Mr. Brady's gallery here, in the city, they tell me, they sent on some of my photographs. On yesterday the principal persons, at the establishment told me they would send you a dispatch to have them destroyed. You will certainly oblige me, by doing so - The only one at all passable, is the one standing, with the large figured dress - back almost turned - showing only side face... This you might retain - On Monday - I will sit for another, which we will send you, if you destroy the others. Please answer -

Very respcty -
Mary Lincoln

Mary Lincoln had no difficulty with the photograph shown here. She is dressed in an elegant gown with her hair adorned with fresh cut flowers. It was taken by Mathew Brady in his Washington studio in January 1862.

Elizabeth Keckly, a former slave who became Mary Lincoln's dressmaker and closest confidant, wrote of Lincoln's comment on seeing his wife dressed in a gown with a low neckline and long train: Whew! Our cat has a long tail tonight, Mother, it is my opinion, if some of that tail was nearer the head, it would be in better style.

Ninian Edwards. Mary Lincoln returned to the home she had first known in Springfield, living in seclusion with the Edwards. On July 16, 1882, she finally achieved her desperate desire to join her husband and lost children, passing away at the age of sixty-three years. Her life had tragedy enough for several people. There can be little doubt that she deeply loved her husband, and both were loving and doting parents over their children whom they adored. To lose three young children and witness her husband's murder embittered her final years.

Below: Mary Lincoln, January, 1862. Photograph by Mathew Brady.

Top Right: Mary Lincoln, November, 1860. Photograph by Preston Butler.

Middle right: The grieving widow, ca. 1869. Photographer and place unknown..

Below right: Ca. 1872, Mary Lincoln was a strong believer in spiritualism. In this photograph the unscrupulous photographer superimposed a pair of hands on Mary's shoulders convincing her they belonged to her dead husband. William H. Mumler, 1869.

The House Divided Speech

*I do not expect the Union to be dissolved – I do not expect the house to fall –
but I do expect it will cease to be divided. It will become all one thing, or all the other.
Either the opponents of slavery, will arrest the further spread of it, and place it
where the public mind shall rest in the belief that it is in course of ultimate extinction;
or its advocates will push it forward, till it shall become alike lawful in all the states,
old as well as new – North as well as South.*

On June 16, 1858, at eight o'clock in the evening, Abraham Lincoln took the podium to address the members of the Illinois Republican Party following his nomination as the party's "first and only" choice to run for the legislative position of senator. In his now famous speech in which Lincoln declared that "a house divided against itself cannot stand," both his enemies and his friends believed the speech was a declaration of war upon slavery in the South. Much of the party wanted to strike a note of moderation in the upcoming campaign with the Democratic candidate, Stephen A. Douglas. Advised to temper his remarks, Lincoln chose to go forward with the speech the way he had written it, unedited.

Lincoln, however, did not view his remarks as "revolutionary." His opponent, Stephen A. Douglas, accused Lincoln of inciting "warfare between the North and the South." Lincoln responded to those who thought his remarks provocative explaining that "I did not say that I was in favor of anything. I only said what I expected would take place."

Whatever Lincoln meant to say, or not say, his words inflamed many in the South who viewed his words as a direct attack on the institution of slavery and a call for its abolition. The perception among pro-slavery people was that any attempt to limit slavery in any way was an attempt to abolish it altogether. They, of course, were right. No amount of explanation or compromise would persuade Southern leaders that Lincoln was content to leave slavery alone where it already existed. In using the phrase "ultimate extinction," Lincoln set the stage for future secession and war following his election in 1860.

"Dividing the National Map." Poster from a series issued by a Cincinnati printer in the summer of 1860.

*And if a Kingdom be divided against itself,
that kingdom cannot stand.
And if a house be divided against itself,
that house cannot stand.*
Mark 3:23-24

Ambrotype by Preston Butler, August 13, 1860.

Illinois State Capitol

A house divided against itself cannot stand.
Abraham Lincoln, 1858

From 1820 to 1839, the state capital was located in Vandalia, Illinois. In 1837, Lincoln along with a group of fellow legislators known as the "Long Nine," successfully convinced a majority of the state legislature to move the capital to Springfield in 1839. During the intervening two years a new capitol was built at a cost of $240,000. It was in this building that Lincoln gave his famous "House Divided" speech in June 1858 pitting the Republicans against Stephen Douglas and the Democrats charging them with a policy to nationalize slavery.

Following his election as president in 1860, Lincoln was given an office in the building, and it was in this building that his body lay in state following his return to Springfield in 1865. During his time in Springfield, Lincoln tried over two hundred cases in the courtroom of the building.

Originally designed to be made of brick, a decision to construct the building entirely of limestone rock from a quarry near the village of Cotton Hill located southeast of Springfield was made prior to construction. The stone gives a distinctive warm buff color to the building setting it apart from the white color of most state buildings.

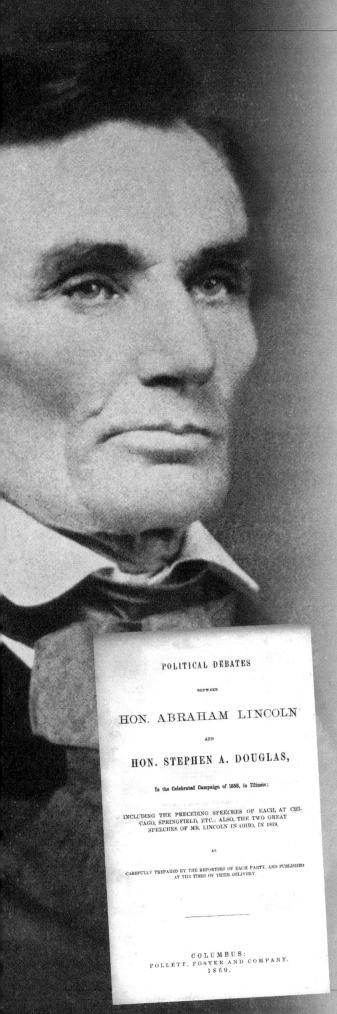

POLITICAL DEBATES

BETWEEN

HON. ABRAHAM LINCOLN

AND

HON. STEPHEN A. DOUGLAS,

In the Celebrated Campaign of 1858, in Illinois;

INCLUDING THE PRECEDING SPEECHES OF EACH, AT CHI-
CAGO, SPRINGFIELD, ETC.; ALSO, THE TWO GREAT
SPEECHES OF MR. LINCOLN IN OHIO, IN 1859,

AS

CAREFULLY PREPARED BY THE REPORTERS OF EACH PARTY, AND PUBLISHED
AT THE TIMES OF THEIR DELIVERY.

COLUMBUS:
FOLLETT, FOSTER AND COMPANY.
1860.

The Great Debates

At the time of his nomination as the Republican candidate for senator, Lincoln was forty-nine years old and had served four terms in the Illinois state legislature and one term as the United States congressman from Illinois's eighth congressional district. The debates came about as a result of Lincoln's efforts to share Douglas's audiences as he campaigned around the state. At first, Lincoln simply showed up where Douglas was speaking and let it be known that he would be speaking later that same day or evening. Then on July 24 he wrote to Douglas asking if he was willing to "divide time, and address the same audiences during the present canvas." Douglas, to his credit as the incumbent, agreed to a joint debate in each of the nine congressional districts minus the two where he had already appeared. Douglas would choose the date and place and set the ground rules. The candidates would alternate the opening and closing remarks at each of the seven sites. There would be a one-hour opening speech, a one-and-a-half-hour rebuttal, and a half-hour final rebuttal. The sites chosen were Ottawa, Freeport, Jonesboro, Charleston, Galesburg, Quincy, and Alton. They began on August 21 and ended on October 15. The debates catapulted Lincoln onto the national political scene, setting the stage for the presidential contest in 1860.

Douglas began the 1858 campaign speaking in Chicago and Springfield, Lincoln's hometown. Douglas's main strategy was to paint Lincoln as a radical closely aligned with the New England abolitionists. He accused Lincoln of altering his position on slavery depending on where he was speaking. Lincoln, on the other hand, tried to show that Douglas's policy of calling for people in the territories to vote slavery up or down would result in slavery existing in perpetuity, becoming "nationalized." While Lincoln suggested the country would become either all slave or all free, Douglas maintained that the country could exist permanently half slave and half free.

When the debates ended in the fall of 1858, Lincoln collected several newspapers that reproduced the debates verbatim. He compiled a scrapbook using clippings from a Republican newspaper for his speeches and a Democratic newspaper for Douglas's speeches in an attempt to insure some sense of accuracy. The Republican Party agreed to publish the debates as a campaign document using Lincoln's scrapbook as the source for the text. Lincoln edited the texts deleting the cheering and various interruptions that occurred during the speeches. Follett-Foster and Company of Columbus, Ohio, published the book in 1860 under the title: *Political Debates Between Hon. Abraham Lincoln and Hon. Stephen A. Douglas in the Celebrated Campaign of 1858, in Illinois*. It became an important part of the 1860 presidential campaign. The book eventually appeared in thirteen editions, selling over 250,000 copies. The editors of *The Collected Works of Abraham Lincoln* used the scrapbook as the source of the text for the debates in their monumental work.

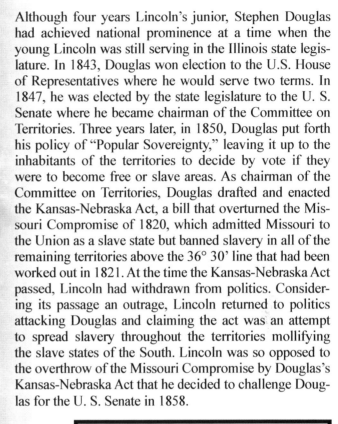

Although four years Lincoln's junior, Stephen Douglas had achieved national prominence at a time when the young Lincoln was still serving in the Illinois state legislature. In 1843, Douglas won election to the U.S. House of Representatives where he would serve two terms. In 1847, he was elected by the state legislature to the U. S. Senate where he became chairman of the Committee on Territories. Three years later, in 1850, Douglas put forth his policy of "Popular Sovereignty," leaving it up to the inhabitants of the territories to decide by vote if they were to become free or slave areas. As chairman of the Committee on Territories, Douglas drafted and enacted the Kansas-Nebraska Act, a bill that overturned the Missouri Compromise of 1820, which admitted Missouri to the Union as a slave state but banned slavery in all of the remaining territories above the 36° 30' line that had been worked out in 1821. At the time the Kansas-Nebraska Act passed, Lincoln had withdrawn from politics. Considering its passage an outrage, Lincoln returned to politics attacking Douglas and claiming the act was an attempt to spread slavery throughout the territories mollifying the slave states of the South. Lincoln was so opposed to the overthrow of the Missouri Compromise by Douglas's Kansas-Nebraska Act that he decided to challenge Douglas for the U. S. Senate in 1858.

The seven sites were distributed from one end of the state to the other. In each of the sites the crowds exceeded the local population. Crowd estimates as large as 25,000 people attended, although both Douglas and Lincoln knew they were speaking to the entire nation.

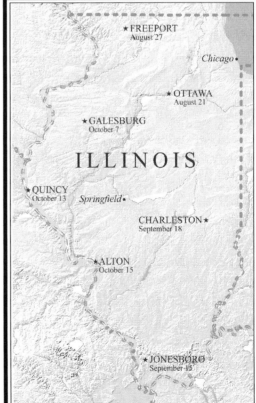

Ladies and gentlemen, I appear before you today for the purpose of discussing the leading political topics which now agitate the public mind. This vast concourse of people shows the deep feeling which pervades the masses in regard to this question. By an arrangement previously made, we have today a joint discussion between Mr. Lincoln and myself as the representatives of the two great political parties in this state and the Union.

I do not question Mr. Lincoln's conscientious belief that the negro was made his equal, and hence is his brother. But for my own part, I do not regard the negro as my equal and I positively deny that he is my brother, or any kin to me whatever.

Ottawa, August 21, 1858

All I have to say is this, if you Black Republicans think that the negro ought to be on a social equality with young wives and daughters, and ride in the carriage with the wife while the master of the carriage drives the team, you have a perfect right to do so.

Freeport, August 27, 1858

The signers of the Declaration were white men, of European birth and European descent, and had no reference either to the negro or to savage Indians, or the Feejee [sic], or Malay, or any other inferior or degraded race, when they spoke of the equality of men.

Jonesboro, September 15, 1858

I say that this government was created on the white basis by white men for white men and their posterity for ever, and should never be administered by any but white men. I declare that a negro ought not to be a citizen whether imported into this country or born here, whether his parents were slave or not. It don't depend upon the question where he was born, or where his parents were placed, but it depends on the fact that the negro belongs to a race incapable of self-government, and for that reason ought not to be put on an equality with the white man.

Charleston, September 18, 1858

Humanity requires, Christianity commands that you shall extend to every inferior being and every dependent race all of the privileges, all the immunities and all the advantages which can be granted to him consistent with the safety of society. Again you ask me what is the nature and extent of these rights and privileges. My answer to that question is this: It is a question which the people of each state must decide for themselves ... Each must do as it pleases. The great principal of this government is that each state has a right to do as it please on all of these questions, and that no other power on earth has a right to interfere with us or complain of us merely because our system differs from theirs.

Galesburg, October 7, 1858

I have no disposition to introduce political and social equality between the white and black races. There is a physical difference between the two, which in my judgment will probably forever forbid their living together on terms of respect, social and political equality ... but I hold that because of all this there is no reason at all furnished why the negro after all is not entitled to all that the declaration of independence holds out, which is, "life, liberty, and the pursuit of happiness." ...

I agree that the negro may not be my equal and Judge Douglas's equal in many respects – but in the right to eat the bread without leave of anybody else which his own hand earns, he is my own equal and Judge Douglas's equal, and the equal of every living man.

Ottawa, August 21, 1858

Can the people of the United State territories in any lawful way, against the wishes of any citizen of the United States, exclude slavery from their limits prior to the formation of a state constitution?

Freeport, August 27, 1858

I do not understand that because I do not want a negro woman for a slave I must necessarily want her for a wife. My understanding is that I can just leave her alone. I am now in my fiftieth year, and certainly never have had a black woman either for a slave or a wife, so that it seems to me that it is quite possible for us to get along without making either slaves or wives of negroes.

Charleston, September 18, 1858

I say there is no way to put an end to slavery agitation among us, but to put it back on the basis that our fathers put it on, restricting it to the old states and prohibiting it in the territories, thus the public mind being in the belief that it is in the course of ultimate extinction.

Charleston, September 18, 1858

These are the two principals that are made the eternal struggle between right and wrong. They are the two principals that have stood face to face from the beginning of time, ... one of them asserting the divine right of kings, the same principal that says you work, you earn bread, and I will eat it, ... whether it comes from the mouth of a king who seeks to bestride the people of his nation, or whether it comes from one race of men as an apology for enslaving another race of men, it is the same tyrannical principal.

Alton, October 15, 1858

Cooper Institute

Lincoln's speech was originally scheduled for Plymouth Church but was changed to Cooper Union while Lincoln was traveling to New York. He did not learn of the change until he arrived at the Astor House on February 25th.

 The reason for the change in venue is not known, but probably made to save attendees the difficult task of crossing the East River to get to Brooklyn during February's inclement weather.

Cooper Union, also known as Cooper Institute. From a stereograph by E. and H. T. Anthony, ca. 1865.
(Author's collection).

Plymouth Church

My wife told me that I must go and hear Beecher while in New York.

Abraham Lincoln

Henry Ward Beecher was one of the most influential clergymen of his time. His sermons were delivered to a congregation that often numbered 2,800 worshippers every Sunday, and appeared in many of the newspapers of the day. Like Lincoln, Beecher strongly opposed slavery, but acknowledged that the Constitution protected it where it existed. He believed that every means possible should be used to prevent its spread into the territories.

Plymouth Church, through its pastor Henry Ward Beecher, was among the more anti-slavery churches in the United States. The church was often referred to as "The Grand Central Station of the Underground Rail Road." So famous was Beecher and his church that people traveling through New York would go out of their way to attend Sunday services there.

Beecher's fame spread far beyond Brooklyn reaching all the way to Springfield. When Lincoln was asked if he would like to hear Beecher preach on Sunday the 28th, he allegedly said, "Oh yes. My wife told me that I must go and hear Beecher while in New York. On Sunday morning Lincoln took the two-cent ferry ride across

the river to Brooklyn where he joined Henry Bowen in his pew. Bowen later wrote that, "The sermon seemed to interest him very much."

From Abraham Lincoln's Cooper Union Address.

You will not abide the election of a Republican president! In that supposed event, you say, you will destroy the Union; and then, you say, the great crime of having destroyed it will be upon us. That is cool! A highwayman holds a pistol to my ear and mutters through his teeth, "stand and deliver, or I shall kill you, and then you will be a murderer." All they ask, we could readily grant, if we thought slavery right; all we ask, they could as readily grant. Their thinking it right, and our thinking it wrong, is the precise fact upon which depends the whole controversy. Thinking it right, as they do, they are not to blame for desiring its full recognition, as being right; but, thinking it wrong, as we do, can we yield to them?

Plymouth Church, located across the East Branch of the Hudson River in Brooklyn. From a stereograph ca. 1865.

The Reverend Henry Ward Beecher. From a carte de vsite, ca. 1865

Matthew Brady Photographs Lincoln
a Few Hours Before His Speech

Matthew Brady, NARA

Francis B. Carpenter, the artist who spent several months at the White House painting the famous scene of Lincoln signing the Emancipation Proclamation, later wrote, "My friend Brady, the photographer, insisted that his photograph of Mr. Lincoln, taken the morning of the day he made his Cooper Institute speech in New York, was the means of his election".

A few hours before Lincoln was to deliver his address at Cooper Union he visited the Bleeker Street Studio of Matthew Brady. Although Lincoln had never met Brady, he was well aware of his reputation as one of the country's most famous photographers.

Lincoln was wearing his newly purchased suit and, although various reports described him as looking somewhat disheveled and tired, he appears every bit the presidential candidate in his well-tailored suit and silk vest. Rather than photograph Lincoln in the usual head-and-shoulders portrait view,

Brady decided to pose Lincoln standing next to a table with his hand resting on a book. Not visible in the picture is a metal head clamp carefully positioned behind Lincoln, supporting his head so that it would remain perfectly still during the long exposure required by the slow speed of the photographic emulsion.

Matthew Brady, NARA

HARPER'S WEEKLY.

A JOURNAL OF CIVILIZATION.

Vol. IV.—No. 202.]   NEW YORK, SATURDAY, NOVEMBER 10, 1860.   [Price Five Cents.

Entered according to Act of Congress, in the Year 1860, by Harper & Brothers, in the Clerk's Office of the District Court for the Southern District of New York.

HON. ABRAHAM LINCOLN, BORN IN KENTUCKY, FEBRUARY 12, 1809.—[PHOTOGRAPHED BY BRADY.]

The Speech That Made Lincoln President
New York, February 27, 1860

*Let us have faith that right makes might, and in that faith,
let us to the end, dare to do our duty as we understand it.*

Abraham Lincoln

Lincoln left Springfield on the morning of February 22nd and arrived in New York three days later on the 25th. The rail part of the trip ended in Jersey City where Lincoln took a ferry across the Hudson River to Manhattan. Lincoln then walked the final blocks to the Astor House (Hotel) where the organizers of his speaking engagement had reserved a room for him. In all, he had traveled just over 1,200 miles aboard five different rail lines sleeping each night in his coach seat.

Lincoln gained national attention as a result of his debates with Stephen A. Douglas in the 1858 senatorial race in Illinois. Although Republican votes outnumbered Democratic votes 125,000 to 121,000 in the senatorial campaign, the Democrats held a majority of the eighty-seven seats in the Illinois state legislature and selected Douglas as the state's senator. Lincoln's performance in the debates, and in the popular vote, elevated him to prominence in the Republican Party.

On October 12, 1860, Lincoln received a telegram from James A. Briggs, a member of the eastern establishment representing a group of New York Republicans who offered Lincoln a $200 speaking fee to appear in Henry Ward Beecher's famous Plymouth Church located in Brooklyn. The reasons for inviting Lincoln to speak were varied; some of the members hoped Lincoln would pull support away from William Henry Seward, the favorite to win the Republican nomination in the upcoming Republican convention in May. Others simply wanted to hear the man who took on the Democrat's leading candidate, Stephen A. Douglas, and won the popular vote in Illinois for U.S. Senator.

Whatever the reason for inviting Lincoln, he was delighted to accept. The fee was the largest he had ever been offered, and most important, it was his chance to show the eastern elite that he was up to the challenge of heading the Republican ticket in November.

Lincoln's theme throughout the speech was a refutation that the founding fathers of the country had not meant for slavery to extend beyond the existing states into the territories and that Congress had the right to regulate slavery with respect to the territories. Recognizing that slavery was a moral wrong, Lincoln told his audience not to be satisfied to seek some compromise or "middle ground between right and wrong."

The climax of Lincoln's speech brought the crowd to its feet, cheering the call to Republican principals:

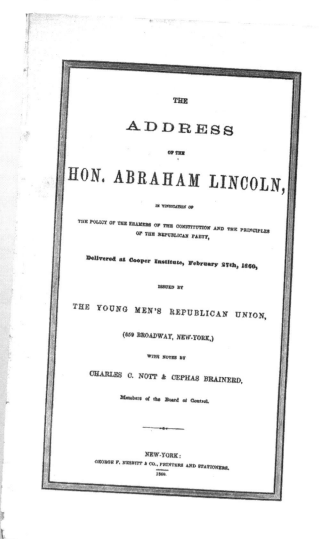

Below: Facsimile of the original pamphlet of 250 copies of Lincoln's speech published in 1907 by Charles C. Nott. Lincoln gave the original manuscript of his speech to Amos J. Cummings, the proofreader for Horace Greely's New York Tribune. Under the title, "Press and Tribune Documents for 1860, No. 1." The Young Men's Republican Union under the editorial direction of Charles C. Nott published the address with extensive notes. The pamphlet was published as a facsimile of the original in 1907 as a presentation gift to the attendees of the Lincoln Dinner of the Republican Club of New York City held on February 22, 1907, at the Waldorf Astoria Hotel.

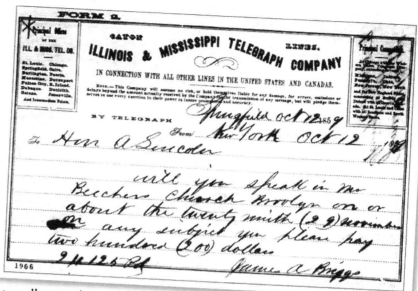

"Neither let us be slandered from our duty by false accusations against us, nor frightened from it by menaces of destruction to the government nor dudgeons to ourselves. Let us have faith that right makes might, and in that faith, let us, to the end, dare to do our duty as we understand it.

Telegram inviting Lincoln to speak at Henry Ward Beecher's Plymouth Church in Brooklyn, offering Lincoln two hundred dollars to cover his expenses. The large turnout caused the organizers to change the venue to the Cooper Union.

Those people who wanted to use Lincoln to pull support away from Seward, giving their own candidate a chance to win the nomination, now had to worry about a rising star from the west. Lincoln's speech not only showed the eastern Republicans that Lincoln was a serious candidate, but that he was now the preferred candidate. As pointed out by Harold Holzer in his definitive study, *Lincoln at Cooper Union*, the speech was Lincoln's last public "campaign" address before the election nine months later.

William Henry Seward. From an unpublished photograph taken by the artist Titian Ramsey Peale at the State Department (June 1863). Author's collection

Lincoln scholar Harold Holzer in his book *Lincoln at Cooper Union* asked what if Lincoln had failed in his attempt to impress the people who attended (and those who later read) his remarks at Cooper Union on February 27, 1860. Holzer writes that it is entirely possible that Lincoln "would never have been nominated, much less elected, to the presidency if not for his Cooper Union speech." The importance of the address cannot be overstated. Lincoln's nomination at the Republican Convention held in Chicago in the summer of 1860 depended heavily on the eventual support of the New York delegation, most of whom were initially supporting New York's former governor and current U.S. senator, William Seward. The anti-Seward forces in New York, and

The elaborate portrait-pin was manufactured as a campaign piece using a Mathew Brady photograph of Lincoln.

Ticket admitting bearer to Lincoln's appearance at Cooper Union (Institute).

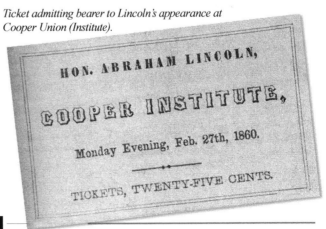

elsewhere in the North, were convinced that if Seward were the Republican nominee he would lose the election to Stephen A. Douglas in November.

James A. Briggs invited Lincoln to speak on November 29, 1859, a full year ahead of the 1860 election. Lincoln balked at the date and asked if he could speak early the next year. An 1860 date would be much closer to the nominating convention and give Lincoln more time to prepare for the all important speech. The committee agreed and February 27, 1860, was agreed upon.

The crowd that came to hear Lincoln on the night of February 27 fell short of the eighteen hundred available seats. Attendees, however, filled the auditorium to just over seventy-five percent, making the event one of the largest to be held at the Institute. Most important, the crowd represented the cultural elite of New York's political society. At twenty-five cents a ticket, the event's organizers were able to cover all of their expenses and come away with a modest profit of just under five dollars.

William Cullen Bryant. Bryant served as editor of the (New York) Evening Post. He introduced Lincoln to the Cooper Union audience the night of Lincoln's speech. Library of Congress

Horace Greeley. Greeley was owner and editor of the influential New York Tribune. Greeley praised Lincoln's speech writing, "No man ever before made such an impression on his first appearance before a New York audience." Library of Congress

Lincoln's New England Tour

The day after Lincoln spoke at Cooper Union he set out on a tour of New England including a visit with his son Robert who was now a student at the Phillips Academy in Exeter, New Hampshire. Lincoln gave eleven speeches in twelve days in eleven different towns between February 28th and March 10th. Lincoln used his Cooper Union text reworking it each time to fit the occasion. The stops included Providence and Woonsocket, in Rhode Island; Concord, Manchester, Dover, and Exeter in New Hampshire; and Hartford, Meriden, Norwich, and Bridgeport in Connecticut.

Lincoln's New England tour served two political purposes. It would enhance his own chances by being seen and heard by so many New Englanders. It would be the last time Lincoln would speak publicly on a political subject before the Republican national convention in May and the presidential election in November.

Robert Todd Lincoln. Illinois Historical Society.

Phillips Academy in Exeter, New Hampshire, in 1865.

Stained glass window in New York Avenue Presbyterian Church.

A Question of Faith

He was not a technical Christian.

Mary Lincoln

Historians have often noted that Abraham Lincoln's knowledge of the Bible is unsurpassed by any president, as evidenced by his numerous references to scripture. While statistics are lacking, it is safe to say that no president surpasses Lincoln in the use of the Bible as a source of material in his speeches and writings. That said, it does not follow that Lincoln was our most devout president, or even a Christian president. Two of his law partners have pointed out that he refused to join any church, did not believe Jesus Christ was the Son of God,

or that he was born of a virgin, or rose from the dead. His own wife affirmed that he refused to become a member of any church, stating that "He was not a technical Christian." And even though his parents were devout church members who practiced the fundamental tenants of their religion, they never saw to his baptism, a failing that placed Lincoln in religious jeopardy by Christian standards.

Lincoln's exposure to religion can be found in the religious practices in western Kentucky in the heart of Southern Baptism. His parents were devoted members of a Baptist denomination known as the "Free Will" Baptists, or "Separatists." These Baptists took their doctrine literally from the Bible and did not believe in the administrative trappings and accoutrements found among other church organizations. They did not subscribe to missionary work, Sunday schools, or financial relationships with like denominations. They believed that every individual was free to associate with the church based solely on the literal teachings of the Bible. The only sacraments they practiced were those that Christ participated in: baptism and Holy Communion, and that only through baptism could one find the blessings of heaven.

Modern First Presbyterian Church, Springfield, Illinois.

Baptism was an essential element of salvation. This was the religious environment that Abraham Lincoln grew up in during the first twenty-one years of his life, so it is strange that he did not adopt the practices of his parents.

William Herndon, Lincoln's law partner and closest friend, described Lincoln as an "infidel." To the Victorian world of Lincoln's day, the word infidel meant "one who is not a Christian or who opposes Christianity." David Davis, Lincoln's campaign manager who was appointed to the Supreme Court by Lincoln said, "He [Lincoln] had no faith in the Christian sense of the word." To those who claimed Lincoln "grew" while in office, his secretary and close confidant John G. Nicolay said, "Mr. Lincoln did not, to my knowledge, in any way, change his religious ideas, opinions or beliefs, from the time he left Springfield til the day of his death."

Lincoln certainly did not oppose Christianity. Although he did not accept Christ's divinity, he believed in and accepted Christ's teachings as a guiding principle. If Herndon was right, Lincoln was not a Christian in the strictest sense, certainly not in the 1860s sense of the meaning. He had not joined an established church, and he had not accepted Christ through baptism. The Presbyterian church that Abra-

New York Avenue Presbyterian Church, Washington, D.C.

ham and Mary attended in Springfield and in Washington, defines baptism as "the act of initiation into the Christian faith and into the Christian Church." To most Christians, baptism was, and is, a requirement for salvation. No baptism, no salvation.

Between 1942 and 1995, several individuals set out to correct this serious omission in Lincoln's life on behalf of Lincoln and their own churches. Lincoln would become a Christian whether he wanted to or not, and the first step would begin with his baptism. And because Lincoln was a private man, his baptism would be held in secret out of public view. The secrecy of Lincoln's baptism protected it from scrutiny, leaving it free from challenge.

It was not until the twentieth century that a series of stories began to emerge that claimed Lincoln had undergone baptism. These stories all have a common thread that runs through each of them. The baptism was kept secret for political and family reasons and was performed by immersion in the Sangamon River near Springfield, Illinois, only days before president-elect Lincoln was scheduled to leave for Washington on February 11, 1861.

The first claim alledging Lincoln's baptism appeared in 1942 in the *Christian Evangelist.* In this claim a man by the name of John O'Kane, a minister of the Disciples of Christ, told of secretly baptizing Lincoln in the Sangamon River shortly after Lincoln won election. O'Kane claimed the baptism was kept secret to avoid an emotional outburst from Mary Lincoln who would have objected to Lincoln becoming a member of the Disciples of Christ.

A second claim appeared in a small book written by Reverend Freeman Ankrum and published in 1947. This account parallels O'Kanes in that it happened shortly after Lincoln's election and was kept secret from the public. Like O'Kane's claim, Lincoln was baptized in the Sangamon River. The only difference between the two claims is the denomination; the

Disciples of Christ versus the German Baptist Church or "Dunkards."

A third claim emerged in 1956 published in *Lincoln's Unknown Private Life*, which appeared in 1994. The story runs the same as the other two. The baptism was performed in secret in the Sangamon River shortly after Lincoln's election. In this instance, the Lincoln family's old Kentucky preacher, Daniel Elkin, came to Springfield to perform the ritual.

The problems with all three of these stories are that the preachers were dead, the Sangamon was frozen over, and the trains they traveled on to Springfield did not exist at the time of Lincoln's election or shortly thereafter. A final point is that none of the preachers themselves ever claimed to have baptized Lincoln; others made those claims on their behalf after their deaths.

The effort to "legitimize" Lincoln in his relationship with Christianity through secret baptism is one of those apocryphal stories that persist in Lincoln lore. There is, however, no evidence that survives serious scrutiny to support the claims of his secret baptism. It simply never happened except in the minds of those people who desperately wanted to save Lincoln's soul, and to make him right with Jesus Christ.

While Lincoln was never baptized nor ever became a

Stained glass window in Foundry Methodist Church, Washington, D.C.

member of a Christian church, he clearly did not oppose Christianity. During his campaign for congress in 1846 he replied to the charge by his opponent that he was an infidel and therefore unfit for public office. Lincoln replied to the charge by writing in a local paper, "That I am not a member of any Christian church is true; but I have never denied the truth of the Scriptures [Old Testament]; and I have never spoken with intentional disrespect of religion in general, or of any denomination of Christians in particular." When asked what his religion was, Lincoln replied, "When I do good I feel good. When I do bad, I feel bad. That is my religion."

Lincoln is perceived as a good man, a man of compassion and great humanity. A man whose life reflected the teachings of Christ as seen in the words "With malice toward none; with charity for all." Although Lincoln rejected Christian canon it appears that he was a Deist who relied mainly on the teachings of the Old Testament. Just as Lincoln considered the Declaration of Independence to be the defining document of the nation, he believed the Old Testament to be the defining word of God. There is evidence that he accepted the teachings of Christ so far as they related to a man's personal conduct. For example, on two separate occasions Lincoln wrote: "I am ... always willing to forgive on the Christian terms of repentance, and also to give ample time for repentance," and, "on principal I dislike an oath which requires a man to swear he has not done wrong. It rejects the Christian principal of forgiveness on terms of repentance." Clearly, Lincoln believed in both forgiveness and repentance compatible with the teachings of Christ.

While references to God are plentiful in Lincoln's speeches and writings, references to Jesus Christ are absent. It is the God of Abraham that Lincoln most often cites. Lincoln's expressions of religious faith go far beyond those of any president in our nation's history. His knowledge of the Bible was exceptional. He quoted from it at length. He used it as a teaching aid to instruct and make clear his ideas. Lincoln's compassion is amply demonstrated throughout the war years. Vengeance and unforgiveness were alien to his private and public practices. He regularly pardoned soldiers condemned to die much to the consternation of his generals, telling them, "I am trying to evade the butchering business lately." When Lincoln stood before the country on March 4, 1865, and said "with malice toward none; with charity for all" he was confessing his faith, a faith that while founded in the Old Testament also found meaning from the New Testament.

Reverend Dr. Phineas D. Gurley (1816-1868)

Gurley was pastor of the New York Avenue Presbyterian Church in Washington, D.C. from 1854 until his death in 1868. In 1859 he was appointed Chaplain of the United States Senate. The Lincoln family attended the church where Lincoln rented a pew. Lincoln admired Gurley's intellect and enjoyed listening to his sermons. On certain occasions, Lincoln attended Gurley's Wednesday evening services sitting in Gurley's office near the door where he could hear Gurley's sermons without distracting the congregants by his presence.

As Lincoln lay dying, Secretary of War Edwin Stanton sent for Gurley to come to the Petersen House and on Lincoln's death asked Gurley to offer a prayer on their behalf. He later accompanied Mary Lincoln back to the White House. On Wednesday, April 19, Gurley, along with Reverend Thomas Hall, pastor of Epiphany Episcopal Church, conducted the funeral service in the East Room of the White House.

Reverend Dr. James A. Smith (1807-1874)

Smith was pastor of the First Presbyterian Church of Springfield from 1849 to 1856. He officiated at the funeral of young Eddie Lincoln in 1850 and became close friends with the Lincolns who rented a pew at his church. Smith left the Springfield church in 1856 over a question of salary. At $1,600 a year, Smith felt he needed and deserved a raise in his annual salary, which the church membership denied. Lincoln's intellectual curiosity and questioning of Christian doctrine led him to read Smith's treatise, *The Christian's Defense*. Although Smith later claimed, following Lincoln's death, that Lincoln came to accept the truth of Christianity, those closest to him denied it. Smith wrote to William Herndon: "It was my honor to place before Mr. Lincoln arguments designed to prove the divine authority and inspiration of the Scriptures, accompanied by arguments of infidel objectors in their own language. Mr. Lincoln gave a most patient and searching investigation... The result was the announcement by himself that the argument in favor of the divine authority and inspiration of the Scriptures was unanswerable."

John Todd Stuart, Lincoln's first law partner and cousin of Mary Lincoln wrote, "The Reverend Doctor Smith tried to convert Lincoln from infidelity as late as 1858 and couldn't do it." It was the intention of some to use Smith to prove Lincoln's conversion, but their efforts failed to achieve their desired results as those closest to Lincoln confirmed.

Mary Lincoln and her children regularly attended Sunday church services, while Lincoln did so sporadically. Still, Smith became a close friend of the family. When Lincoln became president, Smith, along with Mary Lincoln, lobbied Lincoln to appoint Smith U.S. Consul to Scotland. To avoid criticism over appointing too many Illinois friends to government posts, Lincoln appointed Smith's son, Hugh Smith, a Kentuckian, to the position, whereupon Smith assumed the consulship a few years later, following his son's serious illness.

Photographs of Gurley and Smith by John Goldin and Company, Washington, D.C.

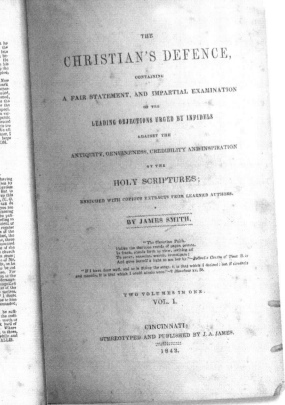

The Christian's Defense by Reverend James A. Smith. Published in 1843, *The Christian's Defense* was claimed to be "a text of apologetics growing out of a debate with the 'infidel' C.G. Olmsted in Columbus, MS, in April 1841." Lincoln's curiosity drew him to Smith and his famous treatise. After reading the book, and despite several discussions concerning the subject with James Smith, Lincoln appears to have remained a skeptic.

Lincoln Runs For President
The taste is in my mouth a little.

With the great success of his Cooper Union address, Lincoln saw his political fortunes rise. An unknown witness to that address told reporter Noah Brooks, "He's the greatest man since St. Paul." Several weeks before the Republican National Convention the Illinois Republican Party declared Lincoln their only candidate for president. Flushed with success and national recognition Lincoln admitted to his local supporters, "The taste is in my mouth a little."

Having successfully moved the Republican National Convention to Chicago gave a tremendous boost to Lincoln's chances of winning. The front runner was New York's former governor and current senator, William H. Seward. Close behind Seward were several prominent Republicans, with Lincoln seemingly bringing up the rear. Lincoln's campaign operatives, however, believed Seward could not survive several ballots. They decided to go after the delegates in Pennsylvania and Indiana who supported Simeon Cameron and Edward Bates respectively, asking them to switch their votes to Lincoln should Seward fail to win on the first ballot. It worked. Needing 233 votes to secure the nomination, Seward polled 173

and ½; on the first ballot; Lincoln polled 102. Seward's failure to secure the necessary 233 votes saw the expected shift toward Lincoln on the second ballot, Seward receiving 184 and ½ and Lincoln receiving 181. Following the second ballot David Davis, one of Lincoln's managers, telegraphed Lincoln who was waiting in Springfield, "Am very hopeful don't be Excited nearly dead with fatigue telegraph or write here very little. David Davis."

The third ballot was all it took, with Lincoln winning in a landslide, 364 votes, 131 votes more than the required 233. Nathan Knapp, chairman of the Scott County, Illinois, Republican Party telegraphed the final results to Lincoln, "To Abe Lincoln, We did it glory to God'. The crowd inside the Wigwam went crazy. Lincoln supporters, who packed the gallery, screamed their lungs out while steam whistles appropriately placed around the convention center blasted the air with their shrill sound. By the next day the eyes of the entire country looked to Springfield and this new Star of the West. Actually, not the entire country. Throughout the South, Lincoln's nomination proved ominous. Threats of secession were already being murmured throughout the land of cotton.

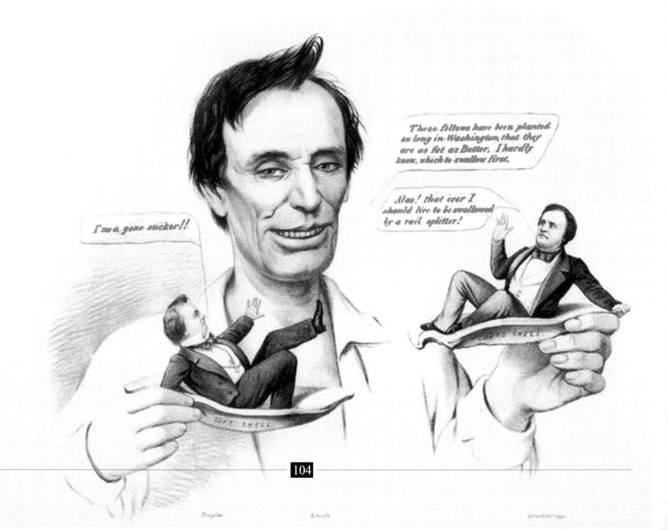

The Wigwam

Chicago was the final selection for the site of the Republican National Convention. Lincoln ally, Norman Judd had secured the city, defeating proponents from Cincinnati. It would prove an enormous boost to Lincoln's chances. Chicago in 1860 was a bustling city with a population of 112,000 people. The city, however, lacked a facility that could handle the large number of delegates and spectators that were expected to attend the convention. The city set about building a convention center that could hold 10,000 people. The building was constructed in just five weeks at a cost of $35,000, most of which was underwritten by the city's business community. The building measured 100 feet by 180 feet, and had a large spectator balcony on three sides. The hall was named The Wigwam, a common name used for large buildings that hosted political meetings.

Although Chicago was home territory for Lincoln, he entered the fray a dark horse behind William Seward of New York and Salmon Chase of Ohio. Despite the large capacity of the building thousands that had gathered had to wait outside. During the balloting, the result of each state as it cast its votes was called out from the roof of the building to the crowd below.

McNally & Co., Sketch by E. Whitefield

Plaque located at the site of the Wigwam on the Worth building on the southeast corner of Lake and Market Streets in downtown Chicago. Following the Republican convention the Wigwam was used for commercial stores until torn down in 1869.

The Wigwam. The special convention center was constructed in just five weeks at a cost of $35,000, most of which was underwritten by the city's business community. The building, which held 10,000 people, measured 100 feet by 180, and had a large spectator balcony on three sides. The hall was named The Wigwam, a common name used for large buildings that hosted political meetings. Wikimedia Commons

George Ashmun of Massachusetts presents Lincoln with the results of the convention nominating him as the Republican Party's candidate for the presidency. The committee met with Lincoln in the front parlor of his Springfield home on May 19, 1860. The diorama is located in the Chicago Historical Society.

Right: *Draft of letter Lincoln sent to the committee officially accepting the convention's nomination. Lincoln sent a differently worded statement to the* Illinois State Journal.

On receiving official notification of his nomination as the Republican Party candidate for president, Lincoln accepted and gave the following statement to the *Illinois State Journal*:

> Mr. Chairman and gentlemen of the committee, I tender to you, and through you to the Republican National Convention, and all the people represented in it, my profoundest thanks for the high honor done me, which you now formally announce.
>
> Deeply, and even painfully sensible of the great responsibility which is inseparable from that honor – a responsibility which I could almost wish had fallen upon some one of the far more eminent men and experienced statesmen whose distinguished names were before the Convention, I shall, by your leave, consider more fully the resolutions of the Convention – denominated the platform, and without unreasonable delay respond to you, Mr. Chairman, in writing – not doubting now, that the platform will be found satisfactory, and the nomination accepted.
>
> And now I will no longer defer the pleasure of taking you, and each of you, by the hand.

George Ashmun

Ashmun chaired the committee that notified Lincoln of his nomination. He would later visit Lincoln before Lincoln left for Ford's Theatre on the night of April 14, 1865. With no time to meet, Lincoln gave him a card that read, "Allow Mr. Ashmun & friend to come in at 9 a.m. tomorrow."

The Rail Splitter.

"The People of the United States are the Rightful Masters of both Congress and Courts."—ABRAHAM LINCOLN.

VOL. I.   CHICAGO, ILL., SATURDAY, OCTOBER 27, 1860.   NO. 18.

The first issue of *The Railsplitter* appeared on August 1, 1860. They ran thirteen issues ending on October 27, 1860.

"This day we unfurl The Railsplitter to the breeze, with what energy and ability we are able to command, trusting that the generous aid and sympathy of Republicans everywhere will rally to our support."

A campaign biography dubbed The Wigwam Edition *quickly followed Lincoln's nomination.*

David Davis

Davis worked around the clock at the Republican convention doing whatever he could to secure delegate votes for Lincoln. On October 19, 1862, Lincoln appointed his trusted friend to the United States Supreme Court.
Library of Congress.

Norman Judd

As a member of the national committee, Judd was responsible for bring the convention to Chicago. He nominated Lincoln at the convention. National Archives.

Leonard Swett

Swett played a major role in convincing the delegates for Seward and Cameron to switch their votes to Lincoln on the second ballot should Seward fail to gain the nomination on the first ballot. Library of Congress.

Election

Well boys, your troubles are over now,
but mine have just begun.

Abraham Lincoln

The presidential election of 1860 was unique among all U.S. presidential elections in one significant aspect – the Republican candidate, Abraham Lincoln, was banned from the ballot in ten of the thirty-three states that existed at that time. The Democratic Party split into Southern and Northern factions, resulting in three candidates. Stephen Douglas represented the Northern faction while John Breckinridge represented the Southern faction. Added to these two factions was the Constitutional Union Party headed by John Bell.

Although Lincoln polled just under forty percent of the popular vote, he won the election by securing fifty-nine percent of the electoral votes; 180 to his opponents 123. He was able to do this by winning the big electoral states of New York, Pennsylvania, Ohio, and Indiana. Even if the Democrats had not split and run their favorite candidate,

Stephen Douglas, Lincoln still would have won the election. The final popular vote was Lincoln 1,866,452, Douglas 1,376,957, Breckinridge 849,781, and Bell 588,879.

Lincoln's appeal covered issues well beyond his opponents. While slavery was an underlying issue, Lincoln's image as a moderate served him well in certain states such as Indiana, while his lifelong support of tariffs made him popular in Pennsylvania. In the end, however, Lincoln's victory made him a sectional winner representing the Northern states against the South. Despite Lincoln's appeal to the South in his inaugural address where he stated that he had "… no purpose, directly or indirectly, to interfere with the institution of slavery in the States where it exists. I believe I have no lawful right to do so, and I have no inclination to do so," the leaders in the South did not believe him. Lincoln's intransigence against allowing slavery to expand into the territories signaled to the South his true policy, abolition. Within a few weeks of his election, secession began and by the time of his inauguration, seven states had seceded from the Union. By May 20, 1861, eleven states had seceded from the Union forming the Confederate States of America. War followed.

Stephen Douglas
Democratic Party
Library of Congress

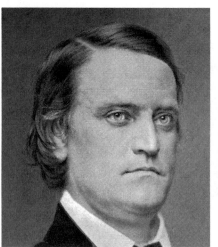

John C. Breckinridge
Democratic Party
Library of Congress

John Bell
Constitutional Union Party
Matthew Brady, Library of Congress

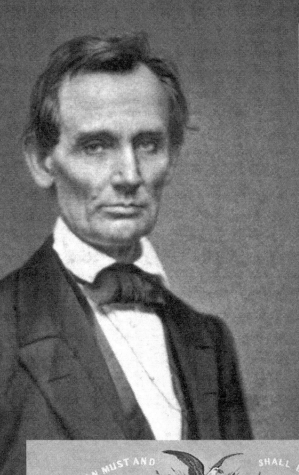

On the eve of Lincoln's election in 1860.   *November 25, 1860. Lincoln's beard begins to show.*   *February 9, 1861, two days before beginning his inaugural journey.*

A Puttin' On [H]airs
The President-Elect Grows Whiskers

Dear Sir: My Father has just come from the fair and brought home your picture and Mr. Hamlin's... your face is so thin.

Eleven-year-old Grace Bedell of Westfield, New York, wrote a letter to candidate Abraham Lincoln one month before the 1860 election advising him to let his whiskers grow because his face was "so thin," adding, "all the ladies like whiskers and would tease their husbands to vote for you and then you would be President." Four days later Lincoln answered the young girl's letter asking her, "having never worn any, do you not think people would call it a silly affectation if I were to begin it now?"

Lincoln took Grace's suggestion to heart and began to let his whiskers grow. By November 25 his beard was clearly noticeable and by the time he left for Washington on February 11, he wore a full beard.

The incident became one of the more enduring stories of Lincoln's fabled life, and it happened just the way Grace later described it. In later life, Grace became the popular guest of honor at many Lincoln functions. During her lifetime Grace received numerous offers to buy the letter, but she simply could not part with it. She kept it in a frame hanging on a wall of her home in Delphos, Kansas, where it stayed until her death in 1936.

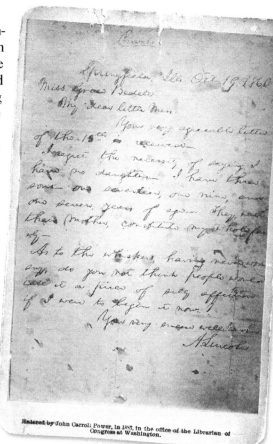

1883 cabinet card sold by J. C. Power, the curator of the Lincoln Monument in Springfield.

> *Springfield, Ill Oct 19, 1860*
> *Miss Grace Bedell*
>
> *My dear little Miss,*
> *Your very agreeable letter of the 15th is received – I regret the necessity of saying I have no daughters – I have three sons – one seventeen, one nine, and one seven years of age – They, with their mother, constitute my whole family –*
> *As to the whiskers, having never worn any, do you not think people would call it a piece of silly affectation if I were to begin it now?*
> *Your very sincere well-wisher,*
> *A. Lincoln*

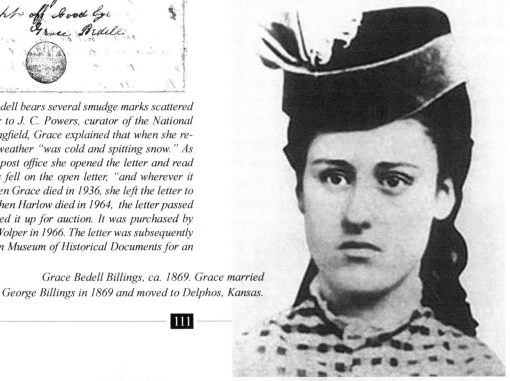

Westfield, Chatauqua Co., N.Y.
Oct. 15, 1860

Hon. A. B. Lincoln,
Dear Sir,

My father has just come from the fair and brought home your picture and Mr. Hamlin's. I am a little girl only eleven years old, but want you should be president of the United States very much so I hope you won't think me very bold to write to such a great man as you are. Have you any little girls about as large as I am if so give them my love and tell her to write to me if you cannot answer this letter. I have got 4 brothers and part of them will vote for you any way and if you will let your whiskers grow I will try and get the rest of them to vote for you you would look a great deal better for your face is so thin. All the ladies like whiskers and they would tease their husbands to vote for you and then you would be President. My father is going to vote for you and if I was a man I would vote for you to but I will try and get everyone to vote for you that I can. I think that rail fence around your picture makes it look very pretty. I have got a little baby sister she is nine weeks old and is just as cunning as can be. When you direct your letter direct it to Grace Bedell, Westfield Chatauqua County, New York. I must not write any more answer this letter right off. Good bye.

Grace Bedell

Lincoln's letter to Grace Bedell bears several smudge marks scattered across the page. In a letter to J. C. Powers, curator of the National Lincoln Monument in Springfield, Grace explained that when she received Lincoln's reply the weather "was cold and spitting snow." As she walked home from the post office she opened the letter and read it. Some of the snow flakes fell on the open letter, "and wherever it touched, left its mark." When Grace died in 1936, she left the letter to her son Harlow Billings. When Harlow died in 1964, the letter passed to his three sons who placed it up for auction. It was purchased by television producer David Wolper in 1966. The letter was subsequently purchased by The American Museum of Historical Documents for an undisclosed sum.

Grace Bedell Billings, ca. 1869. Grace married George Billings in 1869 and moved to Delphos, Kansas.

I bid you an affectionate farewell
I now leave not knowing when, or whether ever, I may return.
Abraham Lincoln, February 11, 1861

A few minutes before eight o'clock on the morning of February 11, 1861, Abraham Lincoln arrived at the Great Western Depot located just two blocks from the Lincoln home. Lincoln and his family had breakfasted at the Chenery House earlier that morning. Although Lincoln had specifically told his associates not to have any demonstration at his leaving, several hundred Springfield citizens showed up to see their famous neighbor off. According to various reports it was either raining or sleeting, with occasional snowflakes. As Lincoln boarded the special coach that would carry him on the first leg of his inaugural journey, he stepped to the rear platform and looked out over the large crowd that stood silent in the rain. As he removed his hat in anticipation of speaking, every man in the crowd removed his hat, a sign of respect for their friend. Lincoln spoke extemporaneously with obvious emotion:

> *My Friends – No one, not in my situation, can appreciate my feeling of sadness at this parting. To this place, and the kindness of these people, I owe everything. Here I have lived a quarter of a century, and have passed from a young to an old man. Here my children have been born, and one is buried. I now leave, not knowing when, or whether ever, I may return, with a task before me*

greater than that which rested upon Washington. Without the assistance of that Divine Being, who ever attended him, I cannot succeed. With that assistance I cannot fail. Trusting in Him, who can go with me, and remain with you and be everywhere for good, let us confidently hope that all will yet be well. To His care commending you, as I hope in your prayers you will commend me, I bid you an affectionate farewell.

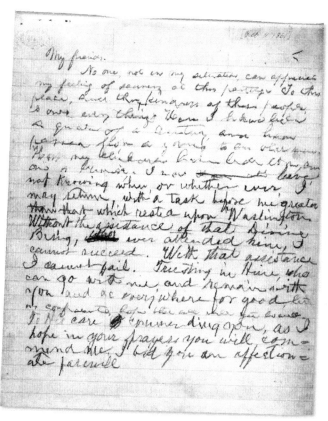

At the request of a reporter Lincoln wrote down his farewell remarks. As the train pulled out of the station his increasingly erratic handwriting reflects the motion of the train as it gathers speed.

Lincoln Says Goodbye

Of all of the scholars efforts to describe the persona of Abraham Lincoln none more clearly captures the nature of the man than the events surrounding a day in January 1861 when the president elect set out to say goodbye to his stepmother at her home at Goosenest Prairie. Having missed the last passenger train out of Springfield, Lincoln boarded a freight train bound for the Terra Haute and Alton depot in Charleston, Illinois. Riding in the caboose, the train pulled into the station late in the evening, leaving the caboose two hundred feet from the passenger platform. The passengers waiting on the platform where the engine stood hissing failed to notice the tall, gaunt figure of a man as he trudged through the muddy ground toward the platform. He carried a small carpetbag belted with a piece of rope securing the contents from spilling out should the latch suddenly pop open.

Abraham Lincoln, president-elect of the United Sates had traveled across the Illinois prairie one last time to visit the one person who had touched his melancholy heart more than anyone else in his life, Sally Lincoln. He would spend his final hours in Illinois with the woman who had not birthed him, but had raised him into the caring and humane person that he was.

Sarah Bush Johnston Lincoln, "Aunt Sally" to most, was seventy-two years old, a widow of ten years. Her sight was failing rapidly and her body no longer able to provide for those around her. Now, in the waning moments of her life, others had to care for her.

Mother and son met in a neighbor's house, thoughtfully provided for them so that they could be together alone during this last visit. The two spent the night sitting before a crackling fire, reminiscing of days gone by and loved ones long dead. Early the next morning they visited the grave of Thomas Lincoln and quietly spoke of times past. When the time came for them to part they embraced one last time. Each suspected it would be the last time they would see each other.

The son gave her a small photograph of himself so she could remember him. Her failing eyes could barely make out the image, but the one in her heart would remain bright until her dying breath. When told her boy had been murdered four years later she would simply say, "I knowed they'd kill him."

The home of Mrs. Reuben Moore, daughter of Sarah Bush Johnston Lincoln and stepsister of Abraham Lincoln. Lincoln visited his stepmother in this house on January 31, 1861 before leaving on his inaugural trip to Washington.

Selected Sources

The subject matter covered in this volume can be found throughout the several issues of the *Lincoln Herald* published by Lincoln Memorial University. The *Lincoln Herald* is one of the richest sources of material on every aspect of Abraham Lincoln's life and death.

Byron C. Andreasen, *Looking for Lincoln in Illinois. Lincoln's Springfield* (Carbondale: Southern Illinois University Press, 2015).

Aden Baber, *A Lincoln With Compass and Chain* (Kansas, IL: Privately Published, 1968).

Richard Campanella, *Lincoln in New Orleans. The 1828-1831 Flatboat Voyages and Their Place in History* (Lafayette: University of Louisiana at Lafayette Press, 2010).

Brian R. Dirck, *Lincoln the Lawyer* (Urbana: University of Illinois Press, 2007).

Frank E. Edgington, *History of the New York Avenue Presbyterian Church 1803-1961*, (Washington, D.C.: New York Avenue Presbyterian Church, 1961).

Lloyd H. Efflandt, *Lincoln and the Blackhawk War* (Rock Island, IL: Rock Island Arsenal Historical Society, 1991).

Jason Emerson, *Lincoln the Inventor* (Carbondale: Southern Illinois University Press, 2009).

Gary Erickson, "The Graves of Ann Rutledge and the Old Concord Burial Ground," *Lincoln Herald*, vol. 71, no. 3 (Fall 1969), 90-107.

Kenneth F. Harper, "Lexington Home of Mary Todd Lincoln to be Preserved," *Lincoln Herald*, vol.72, no. 3 (Fall 1970), 110-112.

William H. Herndon, *Lincoln and Ann Rutledge and the Pioneers of New Salem* (Herrin, IL: Trovillion Private Press 1945).

Harold Holzer, *Lincoln at Cooper Union. The Speech That Made Abraham Lincoln President* (New York: Simon and Shuster, 2004).

Richard Kigel, *Becoming Abraham Lincoln. The Coming of Age of Our Greatest President*, (New York: Skyhorse Publishing, 2017).

Floyd Mansberger, *An Archaeological and Architectural Assessment of the Lincoln Cabin, Rural Macon County, Illinois*, (Decatur, IL: Fever River Research, 2009).

Thomas F. Schwartz, *Lincoln. An Illustrated Life and Legacy* (New York: Fall River Press, 2009).

Edward Steers, Jr., "'A Puttin' on (H)airs.' Lincoln's Letter to Grace Bedell." *Lincoln Herald*, 91, no. 3 (1989): 86 - 90.

Edward Steers, Jr., "Was Mistah Abe Babisized?" *Lincoln Herald*, vol. 91, no. 3(Winter 1999), 164-173.

Wayne C. Temple, *By Square and Compasses: The Building of Lincoln's Home and Its Saga* (Bloomington, IL: The Ashler Press, 1984).

Benjamin P. Thomas, *Lincoln's New Salem* (Springfield: The Abraham Lincoln Association, 1934).

John Evangelist Walsh, *The Shadows Rise. Abraham Lincoln and the Ann Rutledge Legend* (Urbana: University of Illinois Press, 1993).

John Evangelist Walsh, *Moonlight. Abraham Lincoln and the Almanac Trial* (New York: St. Martin's Press, 2000).

Books By Edward Steers, Jr.

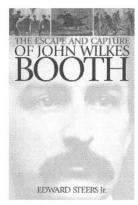

The Escape and
Capture of
John Wilkes Booth

His Name
Is Still Mudd

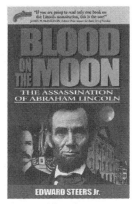

Blood on
the Moon

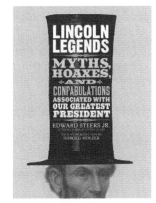

Lincoln
Legends

Hoax

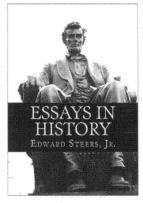

Essays
in History

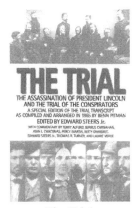

The Trial

Lincoln's
Assassination

Port Hudson
to Cedar Creek

Don't You Know
There's a War On?

I'll Be
Seeing You

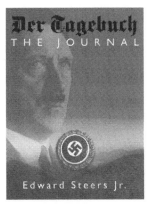

Der Tagebuch
The Journal

Maps By Kieran McAuliffe

 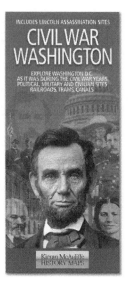  

Folded map measures 5 by 11 inches.

Abraham Lincoln Map   ISBN-13: 978-0986894503

A unique detailed map showing the life of Abraham Lincoln from his birth in Kentucky to his departure from Springfield, Illinois, as President-elect. Every part of his life is covered, including his youth, his life in New Salem, his part in the Black Hawk War, his life in Springfield, and his legal and political career – from state legislator to U.S. congressman, to his attempt for the U.S. Senate and the Lincoln-Douglas Debates, and two years later, to his election as President of the United States. Extensive chronology details the life of Lincoln along with important events in American history.
48 pictures and 3 inset maps. Reading list.

Civil War Washington   ISBN-13: 978-0986894510

Explore Washington, D.C., as it was during the Civil War years. This map shows political, military and civilian sites, railroads, trams, and canals, and sites connected to the assassination of Abraham Lincoln. Detailed index and grid helps you find what you are looking for. Many sites connected to the President are detailed. An introduction to the system of forts that surrounded the city is included.
Over 60 photos. Reading list.

John Wilkes Booth Escape Route Map   ISBN-13: 978-0986894534

Follow the route taken by the assassin of President Abraham Lincoln as he fled from Ford's Theatre on April 14, 1865, until his capture and death 12 days later at the Garrett Farm in Virginia. Completely updated inside and out. Presenting the latest research into the escape attempt of John Wilkes Booth after he assassinated President Abraham Lincoln. Booth's escape route and the search routes are clearly shown and color coded. Follow the fugitives and the soldiers day by day, hour by hour. A 1200-word commentary details the assassination, the escape, and the capture and death of Booth.
34 pictures and illustrations. Reading list.

Raid on Richmond   ISBN-13: 978-0986894527

The incredible story of the Kilpatrick-Dahlgren Raid features all the elements of a Hollywood thriller. Starring Judson Kilpatrick – a cocky West Point graduate and cavalry officer, and Ulric Dahlgren – a dashing blue-blood staff officer who had lost his lower right leg just months before during the Gettysburg campaign. Add a dark and stormy night, a planned but failed prison break, a hanging, an ambush in the dark, a missing corpse, and handwritten notes detailing the destruction of Richmond and the murder of Jefferson Davis and the Confederate Cabinet. A 1200-word commentary details the raid that might have led to the assassination of Abraham Lincoln.
34 pictures and illustrations. Reading list.

LINCOLN SLEPT HERE
LINCOLN FAMILY SITES IN AMERICA

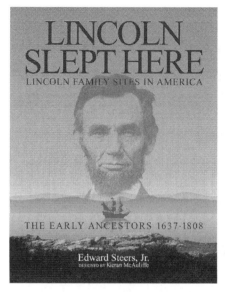

THE EARLY ANCESTORS
1637-1808
Follows the arrival of the first
American ancestor, Samuel Lincoln,
of Hingham, England, in 1637,
to Hingham, Massachusetts, through
the next five generations leading
up to the birth of Abraham Lincoln.

KENTUCKY YEARS 1816-1830
INDIANA YEARS 1816-1830
Begins with the birth of Abraham Lincoln
at the Sinking Spring Farm to the
boyhood home on Knob Creek to the
farm in Indiana where he lived for
fourteen years from 1816 until he left
with his family for Illinois in 1830.

ILLINOIS YEARS
1830-1861
Covers Lincoln's adult years. After
helping his family settle near Decatur,
Illinois, Lincoln arrives in New Salem to
begin his rise toward the presidency.
From New Salem, the newly licensed
lawyer moves to Springfield, establishes
himself as a lawyer, marries, serves
as a congressman, debates Stephen
Douglas, and is elected as the sixteenth
president of the United States.

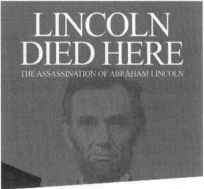

THE PRESIDENCY
1861-1865
Follows Lincoln through the tumultuous
years of civil war leading up to victory
and reunion.

THE ASSASSINATION
APRIL 1865
Within two months of the formal end of
the civil war on June 2, 1865, Abraham
Lincoln is assassinated at Ford's Theatre
by the actor John Wilkes Booth. The
"Assassination" covers the events leading
up to the assassination, the act, and the
escape and eventual capture of Booth.

The
LINCOLN
SLEPT HERE
series is available
at select
National Park sites,
Historic sites,
and on
Amazon.com

Notes